THE SURF TRIP
SURVIVAL GUIDE

**Better be ready
when the shit goes down**

MELANIE & STEPHAN BERNHARD

Snow | Skate | Surf | Streetwear
EUROPE'S #1 SHOP FOR BOARDSPORTS & STREETWEAR
Action Jay: Rod Owen, Lifestyle Jay: Swilly
Lifestyle Justine: Billabong/Sandrine Le Gal,
Lifestyle Marion: Christian Brecheis
O'NEILL
QUIKSILVER
ROXY
RVCA
BILL
Visit us on facebook: facebook.com/planetsports

Teamrider Jay Thompson
Teamrider Marlon Lipke
Teamrider Justine Dupont
Planet-Sports.com
NG   Hurley   REEF   RIPCURL
MORE THAN 450 TOP-BRANDS

IMPRINT

The Surf Trip Survival Guide
Better be ready when the shit goes down

Cover creation: Daria Malek
Conception: Stephan Bernhard
Texts: Melanie and Stephan Bernhard
Proofing & editing: Clark Bruce, www.clarkbruce.com
Layout, design & illustrations: Daria Malek

Copyright © 2012 by Falco Books

First edition
Printing: OrtmannTeam

The original edition was published in 2011: Das Surftrip-Überlebenshandbuch. Better be ready when the shit goes down. © Falco Books, Munich.

Surfing is a dangerous and addictive activity. The authors and publishers take no responsibility for accident or injury as a result of using information contained within this book.

General inquiries can be send to: contact@surftrip-survival-guide.com

ISBN 978-3-00-037562-0

THE TEAM

Melanie and Stephan Bernhard live in Capbreton, just around the corner from La Piste, one of the best waves on the French Atlantic coast. But they have not forgotten how it is to be a land-locked surfer living more than 1000 kilometers from the nearest beach: For many years, their local break was the Eisbach river wave in Munich, Germany, and they had to invest every minute and cent to get to the ocean. On their many surf trips around the world, they did not only score great waves but also got skunked at times and, therefore, know what it takes to be ready when the shit, or ship, goes down. For the rest, the two journalists interviewed surf pros, tropical doctors, crime experts and professional adventurers who shared their knowledge for the Surf Trip Survival Guide.

Being a passionate snowboarder, it was only a matter of time until graphic designer **Daria Malek** tried surfing. Even though her experiences on a surfboard only include a few white water rides at Portuguese beach breaks, the 26 year old is looking forward to her next surf trip. Thanks to her work on this book, she now knows that she will be prepared for anything that could happen on the road or in the water.

WHY THIS BOOK?

The idea for The Surf Trip Survival Guide started four years ago when I returned from a surf trip with my best friend and had to take him from the airport straight to the hospital. It's no exaggeration saying that he didn't look well that day: His entire body was shaken by high fever, the bandage around his wound was drenched in blood and he was so weak that I had to get him a wheelchair. This whole situation could have been prevented if we had known a bit more about reef cuts and tropical infections. But we had no clue and there was no escape route off our road to ruin (the details of this story can be read on page 52).

I then realized for the first time that there are numerous surf guides describing every wave at the end of the world, but not one helps you when your surf trip turns out totally different from what you had dreamt it to be. After all, I had also unnecessarily suffered from a lack of knowledge. An experience that already dates back eleven years, but still gives me phantom pains when recalling this summer day at the French Atlantic coast. On this day I had the misfortune of stepping on a weever (one of these malicious fish that burry themselves in the sand close to the shore and only wait to drive their poisonous stings into your foot). First it wasn't that bad, the pain was comparable to a bee sting, but this was only be the beginning. Soon it was more painful than I would imagine a hornet sting, and the torture didn't end. What I would have given for a guidebook in this situation, telling me to simply hold the foot in hot water for five minutes and everything would be fine (why you can read on page 68). But there was no book like this back then, and it would still take years for the idea to evolve in a cold hospital lobby.

Why should every surfer learn from their own mistakes – isn't it enough if someone else already made them?

Stephan Bernhard

CONTENT

HUMAN CHALLENGES

Humans are like animals, and when it comes to waves they can become real beasts. It can happen to anyone, even the best of us, like Mark "Occy" Occhilupo. Today, the Australian has become one of surfing's legends and nobody would try to teach him a lesson in the water. But things were not always that way: When Mark was 17 years old he paddled out to Sunset for the first time. His big mistake was not kicking out of the wave immediately when another surfer dropped in on him and just continued surfing the wave behind the unknown surfer into the channel. That's where he got slapped in the face for his "disrespectful" behavior. Back in those days they already had a strict lineup ranking in Hawaii, and not everyone had the same right to surf a wave. The same day Mark also got to know the big wave surfer Ken Bradshaw. Bradshaw not only had an impressive appearance, but also had the habit of knocking off fins with his own hands or biting out pieces of the rail of surfboards if he felt offended by another surfer. "I'm still not sure what I did. Out of the blue Ken paddled up to me and bit a chunk out of my rail", Occy writes in his biography.

It is not only locals that can be terrifying and ruin your session, sometimes it is you who is standing in your own light. For example, when the waves are big, but your fear is even bigger. Or, when you miss out on a monster swell because the drinks were flowing like water last night at the bar.

Human challenges can be demanding - you better know how to deal with them.

LOCALS ONLY!

The theory:

"Today, everybody is surfing – moms, dads, sisters, four-year olds as well as grandpas", said the ASP (Association of Surfing Professionals) a few years ago when being asked about the booming surf industry. Some claim that more and more crowded lineups have led to localism. But wait, it is not that simple. Localism has been around since the beginning of the modern surfing era, as an incident in the winter of 1976 proves. Back then, the Australian surfer Wayne Bartholomew was attacked by a group of local surfers in Hawaii. "I lost some of my teeth, my nose was broken and I suffered facial lacerations", the former surf pro recalls. Bartholomew knows why this happened: "I was way too selfish in the water."

In fact, psychologist compare the aggressive behavior by locals with a clan of native people that defend their territory. Locals define themselves as a group through surfing their spot and look at the waves as their property. **Foreigners are seen as invaders** and defending yourself against them, strengthens the group's sense of fellowship like winning a battle. Particularly surfers fighting for the best waves with the locals are seen as "disrespectful" or "selfish" and deserve to be taught a lesson in the eyes of the locals.

Also, new technologies could be a reason for growing localism. A few years ago a lot of experience was needed to be at the right place at the right time. Back then you had to analyze the weather chart in the newspaper to guess if it's worth going surfing or not. Today, numerous internet platforms are offering wave forecasts that get updated every hour; knowing where and when the best waves will break has become a walk in the park.
If checking the web is too much effort for you, you can still stay informed via text message. Consequently the hassle in the lineup is the biggest on those rare magic days – the same goes for the locals' frustration potential.

The daily life:

"It is barely conceivable how an outbreak of violence like this could happen", a Californian judge states after having watched a video. On this video you could see three bodyboarders beating up a surfer, pressing him under water and breaking his board. The judge simply couldn't imagine what led to this violent frenzy. The surfer had only wanted to catch some waves at Fort Point, a spot directly located next to the Golden Gate Bridge in San Francisco.

Surfers who have traveled the world tend to say: **This is normal, you can find localism everywhere.** The only thing different here is that the offenders were sued."

They are probably right, but most of the time violence is not the only strategy locals use. Graffitis like **"locals only"** or **"If you don't live here, don't surf here"** are easy to ignore.

"But if you paddle out and get welcomed with a **'You don't surf here'**, it's a different situation", says the owner of a surf shop in Ocean Beach, California. This happened to him when he wanted to surf at Threes in the Waikiki Bay in Hawaii. Sending foreigners to shore is very popular among locals, but most of the time they only take action after a drop in or some similar "offense".

Often cars with a foreign number plate become the main target for frustrated surfers. In France it is sometimes just a matter of a few kilometers: when you are from Biarritz and surfing in Hossegor, only 20 minutes to the north, you might find your car with four flat tires after your session. On the Canary Island, which is said to have the most aggressive locals in Europe, traveling surfers have already been chased off with stones at some spots. The same might happen if you dare to climb down the steep path to Lunada, a spot in California that is known for its heavy localism – a literal volley of stones might welcome you. Sometimes the locals hit golf balls off the near-by cliff targeting the surfers in the lineup. In Hawaii it might be a direct confrontation when a local is paddling over to you, driving his surfboard's nose into your stick from underneath and shouting: **"Like beef?"** which kind of means "Wanna fight?".

LOCALS ONLY!

Self-protection:
You will find localism on any stretch of coast, but not at every spot.
Beach breaks are always a bit more crowded than waves that are not that easy to access. When you're traveling, you find it easier to avoid crowded beaches while those with a 9 to 5 job have a hard time as they only have a limited time slot. "Giving the locals some free space is one possibility of showing respect", says Mavericks pioneer and big wave legend Grant Washburn.

Even more important is your own behavior in the water. There is nothing easier than incurring the wrath of other surfers. You paddle out with five buddies? You will get yourself in the doghouse even before having reached the lineup. You paddle straight to the peak and take the first wave of the set? Sounds like trouble! Better queue up: position yourself a bit on the verge and let the first set pass through before taking a wave. You drop in on other surfers or you "snake" them, which means that you are paddling around them to get yourself in a better position for the next wave? Do this and you can guarantee a fight! Some surfers think of localism as the only possibility to maintain order in a sport that barely follows any rules, thus banning surfers who ruin the session of others through their behavior.

Therefore, every surfer should ask themselves before paddling out: **"Is this spot maybe out of my depth?"** If it is, you will instantly be identified as the troublemaker. Just imagine the following situation: Somewhere in New York, Berlin or L.A., ten guys are playing soccer in a park. Suddenly four other guys put a soccer ball in the middle of the field and start their match. It becomes impossible to continue the first soccer match, but asking the four guys to remove their ball and place it at a different spot, doesn't work. Their answer: "The park is for everybody." You think this is an unrealistic story? It happens everyday in surfing! For example at a reef in Peniche, Portugal: The spot is located just in front of a big parking lot that is crammed with camping vans from all over Europe during summer time; the consequence is absolute anarchy in the water. This reef somehow draws beginners like moths to a flame. Drop-ins are daily business, often there are even several surfers on one wave, and when a bigger set is coming through surfboards get shot away like flying obstacles. Locals can barely surf here anymore and don't understand why nobody is surfing the beach break only 50 meters away, even though it would be way more suitable for most of the surfers out there.

The Wolfpak is known for defending the waves of Oahu's North Shore against anyone who is violating the locals' rules. Back in the day they used fear and their fists, today their behavior is a bit less brutal, but they are still asking for respect. But what's the best way to show respect? The brothers Kala and Kamalei Alexander belong to the Wolfpak's inner circle, they explain what to expect in the lineup:

"Follow the rules! On a wave like Banzai Pipeline, doing something stupid isn't just lacking surfing etiquette. It's attempted murder. Getting dropped in on at Pipe is like someone pointing a gun at your head. And you know, if you point a gun at one of us, well, there are gonna be consequences. We make sure there's order and that people aren't taking off on top of each other.

If you do drop in on someone, you should paddle to the beach and surf at a different spot. **Leaving the lineup is the ultimate sign of respect!** If you wanna get in trouble, you paddle back out as if nothing had happened.

Patience is also a good thing. It's polite to wait for your ride.

You get what you are asking for. If you are paddling out like a wild bull, you will get taken by the horns. If you hold yourself back, you will be rewarded with a relaxed ride.

Don't just take, also give. You won't regret giving a wave to a local."

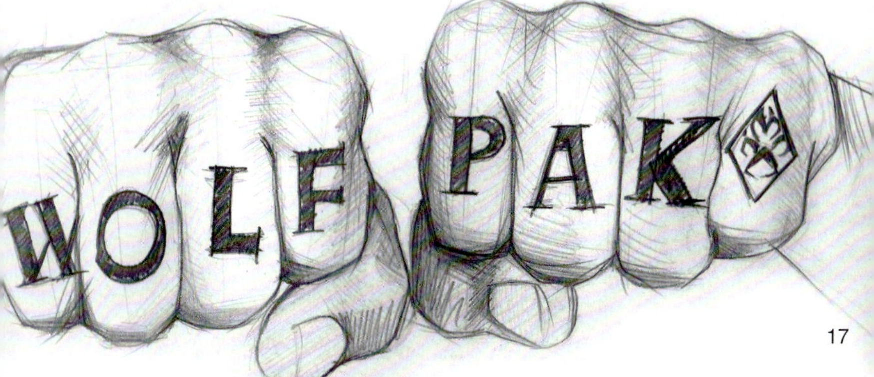

CROWD CONTROL

How many surfers are on this planet? Five million, as suggested by the Surf Industry Manufacturer's Association a few years ago? Or rather 17 million, a number estimated by the Australian Surf Association? Maybe the International Surfing Association is right when they claim that there are 23 million surfers on this earth. Nobody really knows how many people surf, but we all know that surfing has become a trend and that it's getting more and more crowded in the oceans.

When the waves at Lower Trestles, one of the most popular spots in California, are firing, the surfers often wait rail by rail for a ride. The same happens at Snappers in Australia when conditions are good, where 100 surfers or more are fighting for waves. In Europe the lineups are becoming increasingly crowded, too. When the offshore winds blow strong at Fistral, UK's most well-known break, not a single wave on the 750 meter long stretch of beach remains unridden. **Even on Sylt, in the Northern Sea, up to 60 surfers can sit on one bank.** But it is our own fault – or better our DNA's – when a session becomes a mass event.

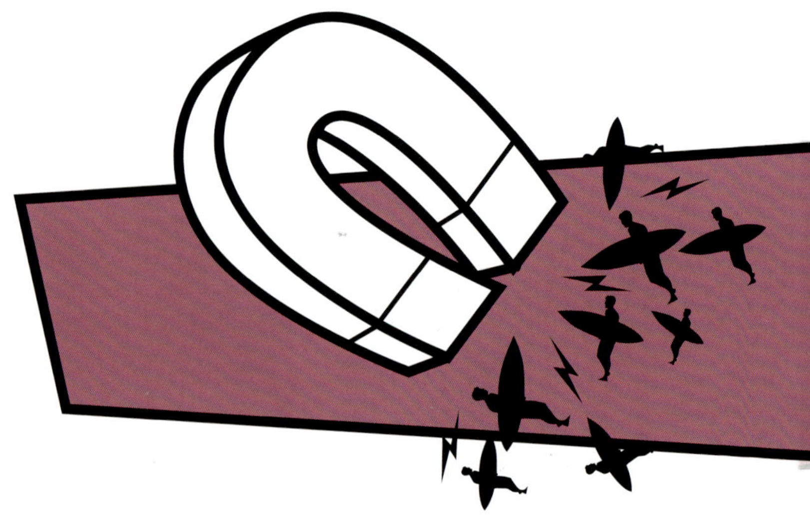

Who hasn't seen the phenomenon of surfing an empty peak on a lonesome beach, when all of a sudden some guys show up in the lineup even though there are plenty of similar peaks all over that place. Psychologists have different theories for this herd instinct that we inherit thanks to our DNA. One of them says: When we arrive at the beach we might not be sure where the best waves break, so our subconscious thinks the other surfers in the water know better and we paddle straight to their peak. However, if this assumption is really true, that's another story.

Opening your eyes is not the only way to handle crowds:

Each of us wants to ride the best and biggest wave of the day, but if 20 surfers are already waiting for the set waves, it might be more fun to go for the smaller waves nobody else wants to take. Surfing's popular, Rob Machado, once said: "Sometimes I surf Pipeline and never end up in the lineup. Every time I see an empty wave while paddling out, I just have to turn around and go for it. There are more empty waves than you think! Sometimes a surfer just bails during the take off, sometimes no one at the peak went for it."

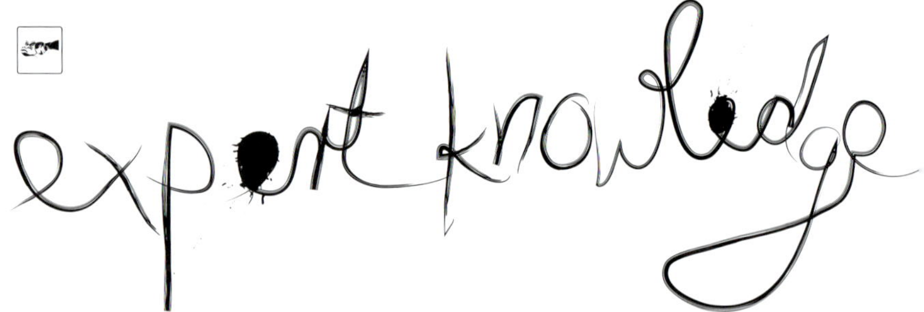

How to surf in one of the world's most crowded lineups?

Jay "Bottle" Thompson definitely knows! The pro surfer from Queensland, Australia calls spots like the Super Bank at Snapper Rocks or Burleigh Heads his home breaks – waves that sometimes attract crowds that would even make Kelly Slater leaving the water like it happened in 2010: "The crowd broke me – I hit two people and got cut by someone else in only 30 minutes", the 11 times world champ recalls.

"When there is a clean six foot swell plus offshore at the Gold Coast, there are 100 surfers already out as soon as the sun rises – surfers, bodyboarders, kayaks and beginners, they are everywhere.

But you can always find uncrowded waves on the coast, it´s not just the Super Bank and Burleigh Heads. If you drive 20 minutes, you might score pumping, lonesome waves. But over the years the coast has been growing – more houses, units, hotels etc. So obviously our population is growing and so is the surfing community. On top of that, the man-made Super Bank has attracted the rest of the world.

Even if it is really packed, usually everybody gets their fair share of waves because there are so many waves breaking, due to short swell periods. Sometimes you get days when it's frustrating and sometimes it´s chaos, like on the day Kelly left the water. But if it´s that crowded I never surf the Super Bank, it's too dangerous.

My best advice for a surfer travelling to the Gold Coast would be: **Paddle out with a smile on your face and** just enjoy how beautiful the coast is regardless if the waves come to you or not. That way you can never have a bad trip to the Gold Coast.

Apart from the crowds there is not much to worry about. The vibe is generally mellow, you get your grumpy old locals at times and there will be a bit of yelling, screaming and a few punches thrown, but it´s pretty rare these days.

I have seen many beatings go down at Burleigh when I was young.
People used to get beaten on a regular basis and admittedly it scared people away from Burleigh, which was a bonus for me being a kid fighting for waves. But these days the police have cracked down with surfing violence and it rarely happens.

The Gold Coast is not like the North Shore. For example, Pipe is generally a nightmare for anyone but the locals. It is an intense and dangerous wave and lot of injuries happen there due to the crowds. **But if you sit on the wave all day you will get a couple of the most memorable rides of your life."**

CREDIT SCORE

This is a true story that occurred on the East coast of the United States in 2009. Two friends were surfing a break by Saint Simons Island for hours. One of them was already back at the beach when he saw a three meter long crocodile headed directly for his friend. The friend managed to catch a wave but the reptile was still breathing down his neck. As the white water closed around the surfer, the crocodile surfaced next to him, opened its jaw and – turned around. But why? The surfer only has one explanation: "That was a warning, sort of instant karma, I´m sure! On the way to the break, I saw a turtle crawling over the street, but instead of stopping and rescuing the animal before it gets run over by another car, I drove on because I couldn't wait to get into the water. The crocodile reminded me to better jam the brakes for a reptile next time." **Imagine what would have happened if he had actually hit the turtle?**

Not every case of instant karma misses catastrophe so narrowly, but the main principal is always the same: No action without reaction, or rather everything you do comes back to you one day. You are dominating the lineup and taking every single wave? **BAD KARMA!** Don´t be surprised if your brand-new board falls off the roof of your car on the way home. You rode someone over in the water and demolished his board, but you don´t want to pay the bill? **BAD KARMA!** It's quite possible that you will find your car broken into and robbed after the next visit to the supermarket. However, instant karma also works the other way: You give a wave to a complete stranger? **GOOD KARMA!** You will be in the perfect position when the bomb of the day is coming through. Pick up some plastic debris from the beach – **GOOD KARMA!** During your next session you will have clean and head-high waves to yourself.

Instant Karma is the "fast food" version of real karma, which is based on the belief of reincarnation and an important part of buddhism and hinduism. According to this belief, every human owns a "cosmic account" that stores their unsolved problems, debts and misdoings. With each new life they get the possibility to deal with these problems and balance the account with good deeds. At some point, says the theory, the human reaches the nirvana, a state of utterly happiness. With instant karma, you get the bill promptly.

FIGHT CLUB 

Sometimes it's not karma, but just bad luck: You are at the wrong place at the wrong time and all of a sudden you are facing a two meter tall Hulk clone who is looking for trouble. Watching him doubling his fists, you know: words won't help here because you will probably take a punch. But, how much the confrontation hurts depends on you and your combat strategy.

Scientists in the US have calculated that a major league pitcher throws a baseball at a speed of 150 km/h to the batter. Thus, the baseball travels the 18 meters long distance between the two players so fast that the batter doesn't even have the time to blink while waiting for the pitch. The blink of an eye simply takes too long – by the time the batter opens their eye, the pitch might already be over. It's the same with the fist of your opponent. The first advice by martial arts experts is: **Never close your eyes and never ever turn your back to your opponent.** Only when you're holding constant eye contact, you have a chance to guess from which direction the next punch is coming and how to avoid it.

If you can't avoid the punch, martial artists recommend a technique that is called "unwinding": instead of throwing your weight against the punch you should go with it. If your opponent aims to hit your face, follow the direction of the punch with your head and upper body – this will weaken the hit's momentum.

If the fist tries to hit your stomach, stretch your abdominal muscles and breathe out in the moment of the impact – this further tightens your abdominals.

If you are not the one who deals out blows, you need to keep in motion all the time – one of the golden rules by professional boxers. Dance from one foot to the other, jump around, do stuff your opponent doesn't expect. If you are lucky, you will confuse your combatant for an instant; this gives you the possibility to counterattack while they are hesitating. Some street fight coaches recommend rattling the adversary with a blood curdling primal scream.

By the way, a black eye is always better than a hook, as hooks tend to lead to knock-outs more often than other hits. So, never give up your guard, always keep one hand in front of your chin and the head slightly down to get this sensitive part of your body out of the target zone.

COUNTERSTRIKE

"I was disgusted and swore to myself to never crash like this again", says surfing legend Gerry Lopez describing a scene, that went down 30 years ago: "And I haven't had one drink since!" By the time Gerry experienced the last hangover of his life, he was already well known for his stylish approach at Pipe and had become a kind of surf star. That's why Gerry came to Hollywood as an actor to play himself in the movie "Big Wednesday" and while doing so, he was enjoying the city's nightlife to the fullest extent – but only up to the day that he took the pledge to renounce alcohol. In the morning a new swell had hit the coast, but Gerry slept in after a long night and when he finally opened his eyes, the onshore had already started. Gerry had missed the session and also drew the necessary consequences.

If you follow his example, you will never again miss a swell due to a good party. But what about those who want to ride some waves after a crazy night out instead of stumbling on shaky legs with a heavy headache and a sick stomach? We have tested the most popular household remedies ourselves:

Water

Theory: Alcohol extracts water from your body, this "dehydration" is one of the main reasons for the rotten feeling the next morning.

Practice: Have a beer followed by a glass of water, do this for the entire evening, and have more water at the end of the night.

Conclusion: It definitely helps! The hangover is merciful and a surf session no problem. The only downer is the amount of fluids that my body has to handle.

Fat

Theory: The more packed your stomach, the slower the alcohol goes into your blood and the more efficient the body can catabolize the toxic agents. Meaning, the greasier and heavier your food, the greater the effect.

Practice: "All-You-Can-Eat-Burger-Night" on the way to the bar.

Conclusion: Showing up at a party with an empty stomach is a classic beginner's mistake. Nothing helps better than a proper meal if you want to go surfing the next morning.

Coloring

Theory: Only dark drinks like red wine, rum or whiskey cause a bad hangover, not white wine, vodka or gin.

Practice: Russian party with vodka on the rocks from early evening until late night.

Conclusion: Early bird session? Never ever! My only consolation: If I had drank the same amount of whiskey, I would feel way worse.

Drinking
Theory: What makes you sick, heals you.
Practice: A small beer after the wake-up.
Conclusion: The hangover fades away with every sip. But no surfing today because the hangover will quickly resurface.

Surfing
Theory: The ocean is like a cold shower, and as soon as your circulation has regained its momentum thanks to the exercise, the hangover will be history.
Practice: Get yourself out of the bed, grab your board and get into the water.
Conclusion: Surfing helps, although each paddle strike feels twice as tiring. My session ends after one hour with a cramp. Notice: Don´t miss breakfast next time, a hung over body is screaming for nutrients.

Magic bullet
Theory: There is one drink that makes all discomfort disappear.
Practice: Fill a big glass with tomato juice, add one egg, some salt and pepper and drink it down.
Conclusion: The feeling of sickness was worse after, than before that special drink. Surfing? Not really.

Salt
Theory: Alcohol flushes minerals out of the body and thus causes a lack of salt.
Practice: Eating! Salty pretzel sticks or pickled herring, whatever you can get your hands on.
Conclusion: If your stomach cooperates, it always helps to have some breakfast the morning after. But it can´t be confirmed nor disproved if a salty breakfast is better than one with low-salt. My morning session successfully started a bit later.

Aspirin
Theory: The classic always helps.
Practice: Watch the fizzy tablet dissolve in a glass of water and pour it down.
Conclusion: There is nothing better for an aching head. But the already stressed stomach reacts extremely irritated – meaning, out of the frying pan and into the fire.

Guinea pig:
Male, mid-30s, 1.75 m, 73 kg, well accustomed to alcohol, had balance problems with each self-experiment

Warning! Each human reacts differently to alcohol, and what helps one person against the hangover, might finish the other person off.

CRISIS AID

One morning you are standing at the beach, the waves look great, but you don't feel like paddling out there – it's as if someone has pulled the plug. You are in a slump and have no idea how to win your stoke back. Even the best surfers sometimes suffer from this kind of surf blues, especially the pros on the World Tour who rush from one contest to the next for years on end. Not to worry, some of them have found strategies to come out of the slump.

The American pro surfer C.J. Hobgood, who did his 12th year on the World Pro Tour in 2011, was asked: "How can you still motivate yourself after such a long time?" His answer: **"I make sure I'm still having fun.** This works with little changes that I try every year. For example, hiring a new coach, surfing new boards, bringing my family with me to events or leaving them at home – that's how I keep the tour new and interesting for me. If you just repeat the same routine over and over again, you will find yourself burned out pretty soon."

Where routine reigns, boredom is born and kills any motivation.
Fight against this vicious circle is not only essential for pros, but for any surfer. You do the same trip every year? Maybe you have forgotten how exciting it is to discover a new spot. You only go surfing when the conditions are perfect for your shortboard? Why not try a longboard, or a fish from time to time? You will be surprised about this new feeling of gliding down a wave.

"One thing that stops people from trying new things is the fear of failure", says surf legend Laird Hamilton. "I don't understand why we always think that we need to be perfect once we are grown up, kids fall all the time and laugh about it. Learning something new, you will force your mind to face new challenges. You have to fail to succeed, that's part of learning."

Frustration is another downer every surfer knows, no matter if they are a pro who gets kicked out of the contest in the first round or a beginner who experienced nothing but wipeouts during the last session. Joel Parkinson narrowly missed the World Champion title a few times and knows what frustration looks like: "After four or five contests some surfers begin to get frustrated", the Australian explains. "They start seeing only the negative side of things. Few of them even become ticking time bombs and explode for trivial reasons, others keep their frustration bottled up. But on the World Tour there is no place for negative thoughts – as soon as you start thinking like this, you are not playing in the upper league anymore. I try to see every situation as something positive. If there are no waves, I'm glad to get a day of rest."

Positive thinking is the key: You can scream out your frustration about a crowded point break, or tell yourself that there is certainly a wave out there which is worth getting in the water for. "Everybody gets what they deserve. If you are looking for trouble, you'll get into trouble. If you just want to have a good time, you'll have a good time. It all just depends on your attitude", knows Laird Hamilton.

PSYCHOANALYSIS

One look at the snapped board and you are done. As you see the lacerated, broken pieces of foam and fiberglass floating in the water, you slow down. The energy that you felt while running down the beach is gone. You already knew yesterday that today would get big, bigger than anything that you have ever considered to be in your "comfort zone", but you have always dreamed of riding waves like these: steep, hollow barrels, breaking over the reef with mechanical precision. Just in front of you, other surfers score perfect rides while you are... scared. **Lady Fear has got you: the only hurdle between you and the waves of your dreams. But how do you conquer her?**

Californian pro surfer Keith Malloy is in his mid-thirties and has spent so many hours in the ocean that he forgot how to be scared. The constant confrontation with mountains of water has made him so self-conscious that he doesn´t fear any wave. Still, he knows exactly how to keep control of your head: "Don´t think too much! Try to eliminate everything that makes you scared in your head. If you constantly think about what could happen and imagine one worst-case scenario after the next, you just get crazy and intensify your fear."

Soul surfer David "Rasta" Rastovich says that accepting the fact that we are never in full control of all eventualities is the best advice: "Even when we sit in a car, we are only in control of our own vehicle, not of all the traffic or of another driver who could run into us. Should we therefore be afraid of driving? No! The same with surfing, every one of us falls or gets washed by a big wave. But in most cases we are kept under water for no longer than 20 seconds. **If you stay calm, you can hold your breath without problems. But if you panic, you will struggle for air within seconds.** You need to accept wipeouts as part of surfing, that's the trick. For what is normal, doesn´t scare you."

Laird Hamilton, who is surfing waves that do not accept a single mistake, says that fear can even have advantages: "She can paralyze and destroy you or help you, you just need to know how to use her. **Fear has a stronger effect on your body than any drugs.** You think faster, react more precisely, I would even say: You are stronger. Learn how to use your fear: go diving with sharks if they are your worst nightmare, or climb mountains if you are afraid of heights, thus you will get used to the feeling of fear."

In case you are actually in a dodgy situation, for example your leash has been ripped and you get washed away by a strong current, a simple trick will help you to avoid panic. It is so effective that it is even part of the training of Navy Seals and other American special forces and helps them to stay calm in combat situations: **Just deeply breathe in for five seconds, then hold your breath for five seconds and breathe out for another five seconds** – your mind will be much clearer, and you will be able to think rationally again.

GAMEPLAN

On February 13, 2010, Californian surfer Shawn Dollar took off on one of the biggest waves a human being has ever paddled into: a 55 feet, or 17 meters, monster which broke in Mavericks, America's most famous big wave spot. However, Shawn didn't accomplish this heroic deed overnight, he got himself prepared and this took him three long years.

"Every night, before falling asleep, I repeated the same sentence: 'There is a huge storm spinning out in the Pacific Ocean which is sending massive waves into my direction. One of these waves is bigger than the others and only made for me. I will surf this wave'", Shawn recalls his mental preparation for D-Day. "Like this, the wave had already existed in my head for many years before it actually showed up in reality that day in February. When this happened, I was really surprised how it all came about just like I had imagined it so many times: When the wave raised in front of me, I didn't hesitate for a second, but just surfed this massive mountain of water as relaxed as I had always done it in my meditations. Everybody knows that professional athletes not only train their body, but also repeat their motion sequences in their heads over and over again. That's how I did it with this wave for three years – I was kind of obsessed by it and now, after it's all done, it almost feels like salvation."

If you don't want to break any records on your surfboard, you don't have to plan the next session as far in advance as Shawn did, but the right preparation can be the key to your success. When a new swell hits Mavericks, even the most experienced locals don't paddle out without giving it a thought. They examine the situation, counting the waves per set, memorizing the biggest

ones, checking on the frequency of the freak sets and if the faces of the waves are clean or a bit bumpy, and much more. They do this for just one reason: to know where they should be positioning themselves in the lineup that day. In the end, nobody likes to get eaten by a two-story high white water foam ball.

At a risky spot, a surfer should not only memorize any details, but also think about what could happen. Imagine the worst-case scenario and mentally prepare yourself for it, otherwise you might all of a sudden find yourself being confronted with an unknown situation. If so, an almost harmless situation can turn into a critical one and a critical one into your biggest nightmare. **"The preparation makes the difference"**, also knows big wave pro Mark Healey whose preparation can sometimes be quite exceptional, as a day in Puerto Escondido proved. Mark was on his way into the lineup, when he got washed in by a huge set and lost his board while being tossed underwater like in a washing machine – his leash simply couldn't bear the impact and broke, but swimming to shore was impossible due to strong currents. "It's kind of strange but the evening before I just had imagined what to do in a situation like this. I thought it would be the best to swim to the open ocean and wait for one of the fishing boards", he says. "I even had put 100 pesos in the pocket of my boardshorts for a little persuasion to give to the captain." After about half an hour of treading water out at sea, Mark got picked up by a Mexican fisherman and got a lift back to the beach.

BOMB THREAT

Every surfer dreams about it: paddling into a big wave. For Mark Healey, this is everyday life stuff. The Hawaiian pro surfer drops into 40 feet giants without batting an eyelash and tells us how everyone can outgrow their own personal limits.

"It's all about your mind. When the horizon darkens and one of these giant, deepwater swells is standing up in front of you, your first instinct is to paddle for your life. If you follow your instinct, you'll most probably never catch one. But actually it is pretty simple:

Lesson 1:
Dupe your brain. Hold your spot when everyone else is scrambling. When it looks like you're going to be the only one to get it on the head, that's usually the place you need to be. Of course, every once in a while, the ocean plays a trick on you, but hey, in life it's about taking risks all the time.

Lesson 2:
Don't hesitate. If you decide to go for a wave, go for it. There's a certain thing that kicks in me when I decide to go, and my mind doesn't set in until I'm cannon balling or sticking the drop. Never ever decide mid-lip that you made a bad call and then try to take it back.

Lesson 3:
Take an extra stroke. The bigger the waves, the more difficult they are to surf. There is so much water and wind moving up the face that it will easily flick you off if you don't give yourself that extra insurance.

Lesson 4:
Don't look down. It never looks like you can make it when you look down this long vertical face. You will surprise yourself as long as you believe you can.

Lesson 5:
If you fall, try again. You got caught in the washing machine? Don't think too much about it and get out there again. In the end it's only water!"

NATURAL NIGHTMARES

Nature is a feisty diva. As soon as she has lured you with her charm, she brings out the claws. It can happen out of the blue, all of a sudden and without any warning. Never feel too confident, no matter how stunning the panorama – this is what skipper Klaus Baumgartner had to learn the hard way when he navigated his surf charter boat to the remains of the Krakatau, an Indonesian volcano. In 1883, there was an enormous explosion here – so loud that the bang was even heard in Perth, 3100 kilometers away. The power of the volcanic eruption extinguished 165 cities and villages as well as the volcano island itself that almost completely sunk into the ocean.

Today, parts of the island have surfaced again since the volcano has started reemerging in 1927. Skipper Klaus dropped the anchor to go on a little excursion on the island – even though wads of smoke were coming out of the volcanic vent. Klaus, who has been cruising from spot to spot in Indonesia with traveling surfers for many years had already seen this phenomenon a few times. He didn't see any need to get worried. Once the small group arrived on the shoulder of the volcano, it became evident that the mountain was capable of doing more than just producing smoke: The ground was littered with black rocks that must have fallen from the sky. Some were only as big as a fist, others had the dimensions of a fridge and had driven deep craters into the ground. Nobody knew if this had occurred a decade or only ten days ago, but when the group of surfers had reached the area just underneath the volcanic cone, a literal desert of rocks without any vegetation, they suddenly found themselves in the middle of a disaster: There was a detonation, boulders flying, panic evolved and everybody started running! After a few meters, Klaus stopped. "When I don't see what's coming, I can't really dodge" crossed his mind and he forced himself to stay and turn around. What he saw almost skipped his beat: rocks were flying through the air, one missed two of the fleeing surfers by only a few meters, but Klaus was lucky – none got really close to him.

It's not only volcanos that can be feisty. Sometimes it's an earthquake, the hardest wipeout of your life or a sharp coral that all of a sudden renders your once relaxed day into a struggle for survival.

Nature can be a nightmare – remember some ways to escape, just in case...

SURPRISE RISK

Some surf trip destinations might offer more adventure than you are looking for.

Java, Sumatra or Mentawai Islands

Indonesia is one of the most seismic prone areas on the planet. In 2010, the earth shook three times here with a magnitude of 7.2 to 7.8 on the Richter scale, which causes buildings to collapse. Since 2000, Indonesia has experienced 15 major earthquakes. Most of the times the epicenter is in the Sunda Trench that is directly off the coast of Java and Sumatra; therefore, both islands are greatly endangered. Most boat trips to the Mentawai start from the city of Padang on Sumatra that was devastated by a heavy earthquake in September 2009; more than 1000 people died. Tsunamis are another threat often caused by an earthquake. In October 2010, a surf charter boat anchoring off an island in the Mentawai was hit by a tsunami and got washed into the jungle.

Caribbean Sea or Florida

Statistically, six hurricanes leave a path of destruction every year. Sometimes it is less, sometimes more, like in 2005 when 15 hurricanes ravaged the Caribbean Sea. Four of them were even classified as hurricanes of the category 5. When such a storm hits the coast with an average wind speed of more than 250 km/h, streets get flooded, ships get washed inland from the harbor into the cities and houses razed out of the ground. In Puerto Rico, the probability to meet a hurricane is the greatest, followed by the Dominican Republic, Cuba, the Bahamas and the southern tip of Florida. Also Barbados and Jamaica have been hit by hurricanes, but the chances are lower. The most dangerous month is September, with more than one third of all hurricanes happening, followed by August and October, each representing one fifth of all hurricanes. The official hurricane season starts on June 1st and ends on November 30th. However, there is no security guarantee for the rest of the year: In 1955, hurricane Alice hit the islands of the Lesser Antilles in the South Caribbean Sea between January 1st and 6th.

Japan

If you plan a trip to Japan, stay away from Tokyo: The probability that the metropolis will be hit by an earthquake with a magnitude of 7 on the Richter scale in the next 50 years is 90 percent. At least that was the forecast made by Japanese scientists in 2004; they had analyzed all earthquakes in Japan within the last 120 years and calculated the probability for the next big one based on their results. The devastating earthquake that was followed by a tsunami in March 2011 hasn't changed this outlook as the catastrophe was emanated from another fault line.

California

The Golden State, too, is still waiting for "The Big One". The Southern California Earthquake Center forecasts that the probability that a major earthquake of the magnitude 6.7 will hit by 2038 is 99.7 percent. The probability for an even heavier earthquake with a magnitude of 7.5 is 46 percent. The reason for this is the numerous geological fault lines underneath the earth. Scientists compare the situation with a burst glass panel that is swept with cracks. One of these imbalances, the San Andreas Fault, statistically causes a major earthquake every 150 years but nothing has happened in 300 years– an earthquake is more than overdue.

One thing that happens with utmost certainty every year between July and October in California: the heavy forest fires. Especially when the Santa Ana winds inflame the fires with gusts of more than 140 km/h, parts of California turn into a burning hell; in some years, thousands of houses fall prey to the flames and entire cities need to be evacuated.

Chile

In 1960, an earthquake with magnitude 9.5 hit the country – the heaviest seismological activity ever recorded. This is not an exception in this area of the planet: Chile has been hit by some of the world's heaviest seismic shocks, for example in February, 2010, when an earthquake with a magnitude of 8.8 caused houses to collapse, triggered a tsunami, cut off the electricity nationwide and left the country in a state of chaos for days. Due to the movement of the tectonic plates, entire villages were displaced: The city of Concepción, which was not far from the epicenter of the earthquake, was moved three meters to the west. Some scientists believe that the earth's crust has not released tensions since then; therefore, the potential for further major earthquakes in the region has not decreased, but grown.

DISASTER TACTICS

"It won't happen to me", you think? But what happens when you're wrong?

Earthquake
What it's about: Deep beneath the earth's surface tensions slowly build up, release and make the ground shake. Often it's only lamps swinging, sometimes books and dishes fall off shelves and in rare cases you can hardly stay on your feet. From 5 or 6 magnitude earthquakes on, buildings get damaged. In these cases, the released energy is comparable with the explosion of the Hiroshima nuclear bomb. Every year there are about 800 of these earthquakes. Fortunately, it only happens once a year that a seismic shock exceeds a magnitude 8 that sets free energy equating to 1200 nuclear bombs.

Don't: Run outside. It's not the earthquake that kills, but the debris – bursting windows or collapsing walls.

Do: Crouch under a table, protect your head with your arms and wait. If you are outside, stay away from buildings and things like electricity towers.

Tsunami
What it's about: First, the ocean draws back, then the nightmare either hits in form of a breaking wave or an immediate rise of the sea level. Even two meter high tsunamis can pave their way hundreds of meters inland.

Don't: Wait at the beach until the sea comes back. A tsunami strikes out of the blue, floods buildings within seconds and transforms streets into rapid rivers.

Also not a good idea: Thinking that the danger is over after the first wave, most of the times a few waves follow in a row.

Do: Run! Run away from shore to the highest elevation in the area – if you have no other possibility, get on the roof terrace of the next resort. Become cautious if dozens of cockroaches start coming out their holes or elephants try to break free. It's not scientifically proven that animals can feel an impending tsunami, but stories from eyewitnesses imply this suggestion. More reliable is a tsunami warning via text message: Simply sign up on www.tsunami-alarm-system.com and never turn your cell phone off during your vacation.

Hurricane

What it's about: A category 2 hurricane with a speed of 160 km/h can twist trees, uncover roofs, push over cars and transform tiles, bikes and fence posts into deadly missiles. With more than 300 km/h the gusts of a category 5 hurricane can sweep away entire buildings.

Don't: Wait for the arrival of the storm at the beach. Even more dangerous than the extreme gusts are the huge tidal waves a hurricane produces. Nine out of ten hurricane victims drown.

Do: Escape inland and entrench yourself in a room without windows. Fortunately, hurricanes never come out of the blue. When there is a threat everybody learns about it in time – not matter if tourist or local.

Volcano

What it's about: 1000°C hot clouds of ember that race down the shoulders of a volcano with 800 km/h, red-hot rivers of lava, ash fall and volcanic bombs – boulders weighing tons falling down from the sky.

Don't: Waste time.

Do: Escape! Nothing on this earth can withstand the powers of an unleashed volcano.

Wildland fires

What it's about: Temperatures from 800 to more than 1000°C and 50 meter high fire walls that pave their way through forests with 10 to 20 km/h and can even jump over rivers and streets.

Don't: Try to escape by foot without a plan and a goal. The danger to get outran by the fire is too big. Australian firefighters know: "Don't run for your life, because you often run straight into death."

Do: Stay in the house. Often a fire moves so fast over a building that you get spared inside. It's also safer to stay in the car than escape by foot. Turn the car directly towards the fire, shut down the AC and crouch yourself on the floor – contrary to movies, cars don't explode in reality. If you get caught by foot, you can only throw yourself on the ground – ideally on a street – with your head down and pray.

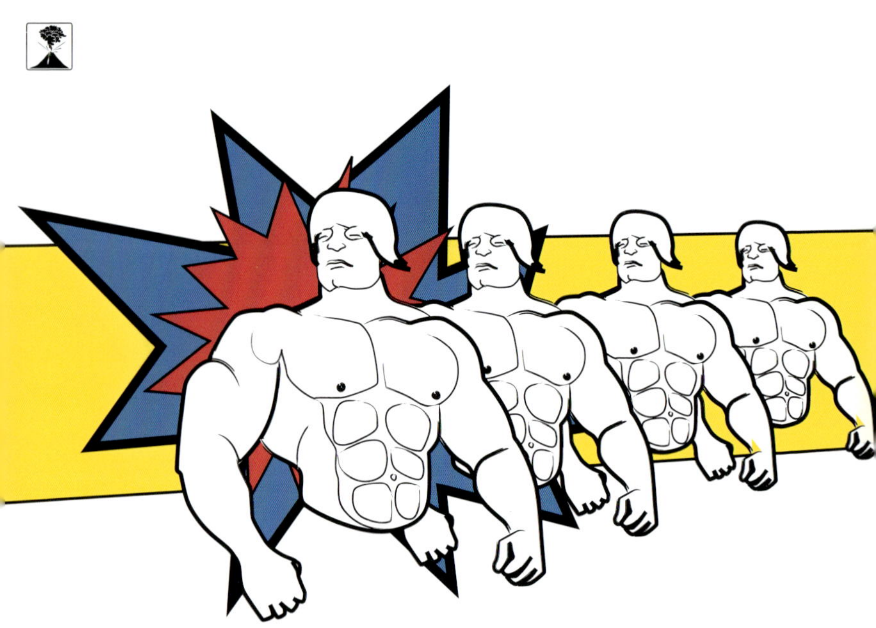

CATASTROPHIC REACTION

It's not only luck or bad luck when it comes to surviving a catas-trophe.

Brainless forces

When confronted with a dangerous situation, adrenaline is released, blood gets pumped into the muscles and breathing accelerates. In short: When facing a combat, the body turns on its turbo charger and is ready to unleash supernatural power or to sprint faster than ever before. Perfect when you have to defend yourself against an angry bear, but in case you need to find the way out of a burning house you're badly off as logical reasoning doesn't really work anymore in this condition.

Deadly freeze

It happens during any big disaster: Some people seem to freeze in the midst of the chaos and don't even try to leave the sinking ship or the burning club. They surrender to their destiny and are incapable of taking any action. This behavior is also probably pre-programmed in our DNA. For our ancestors it might have made sense to throw themselves on the ground and pretend to be dead when facing a predator. But today we are confronted with so much stress that we don't know what to do anymore, it is possible that our brain recalls these ancient behavior patterns – in the worst case we stop right on the tracks while a train is approaching instead of just simply jumping to the side.

Smart steps

"Breathe, plan, act", says the 3-step-survival plan. If you force yourself to breathe slowly, you will calm down instantly and delay upcoming panic. Next, you should realize your situation. For example: "My ship is sinking!", make a plan of what to do next. Plan in small steps, don't think "I have to save myself". Instead, take it one by one: "I'm searching for a stairway", "I must go on deck", "I must find a rescue boat"... If you force yourself to think in small steps, you have to think logically and this controls any upcoming feeling of panic. Finally, you only need to follow your plan step by step.

SOLAR POWER

The sun warms you up when you're cold, but if you don't watch out, the solar rays can make your life miserable.

A lesson two Germans learned not even 24 hours after they had arrived on the Caribbean island of Isla Margarita. Nothing seemed to be more alluring than getting a bit of sun after the long flight, their only mistake was going to the beach around lunchtime. An idea that would leave the Public Health Portal of the European Union in disbelief. Their recommendations for a place close to the equator: avoid the sun during noon, stay in the shade, wear a t-shirt and hat, and apply sunscreen.

At least the two friends applied sunscreen before getting roasted in the sun. The down side, sun protection factor (SPF) 2 is way too low for a 2 hour-sunbath. Despite their slightly burned and red colored skin, they weren't too worried about their condition in the evening – in the end it was only a sunburn, right? But the next morning was different: it started with a yell and pain of unknown extent.

One of the tormented tourists crawled from the bed to the window and pulled back the curtain. A huge mistake: As soon as one of the sun rays had hit his skin, the pain flooded his entire body. It felt as if the sun's rays were splatters of boiling water. The only cure were three days in a dark room with the curtains closed, but still their skin was so hot that they could have easily melted a piece of butter on their foreheads.

A painful experience that could have been avoided if they had only considered a few tips:

Sunscreen with SPF 2 might have been sufficient on a spring day somewhere in Northern Europe, but never on a beach in the Caribbean. The reason is the

UV index, a worldwide valid chart that indicates with how much power the sun burns down on us. A winter day in Germany is rated 1 to 2 and is considered harmless. Even the German summer doesn't exceed a value of 8, which means that **you shouldn't go tanning during lunchtime and apply at least SPF 15.** But in the Caribbean, values beyond 11 or 12 are normal – the sun becomes an enemy you can't fight.

Every sunscreen has its limits and no product offers 100 percent protection. In the European Union, the term "sunblock" has been forbidden, in the United States the same goes for "all day protection". Both terms are misleading because nobody can expose themselves to the sun all day without any worries, no matter which sunscreen they are using.

Just as well, a sunscreen with SPF 30 doesn't offer twice as much protection as SPF 15. In fact, SPF 10 blocks 90 percent of the solar radiation, SPF 15 blocks 93 percent and SPF 30 blocks 97 percent. With 98 percent, even SPF 50 barely offers more protection. However, how long the sunscreen saves you from getting sunburned mainly depends on your skin type.

Wearing a white t-shirt in the water still exposes you to 10 percent of the solar radiation. Also, palm trees are not a perfect shelter because 50 percent of the sun rays will still find their way onto your skin. Even the deepest tube doesn't offer you a breather from the sun; the water tunnel will only absorb half of the rays.

Most important for surfers is the term "waterproof". By definition it is sufficient if the sunscreen provides 50 percent of its protection after 40 minutes in the water; given this, the sunscreen can claim the term "waterproof". But what is left after a two-hour surf session?

Don't forget that sunscreens have a due date, just like food! Rather buy a new one each season.

A good sunscreen should not only contain UVA and UVB filters, but also titanium dioxide and zinc oxide that reflect the sun rays and block them from your skin.

FROST PROTECTION 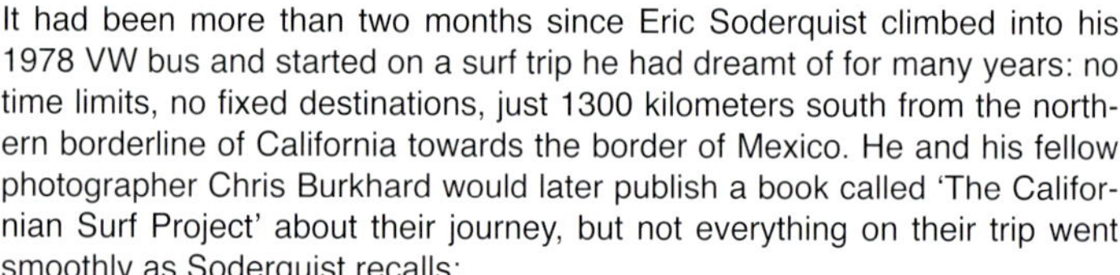

It had been more than two months since Eric Soderquist climbed into his 1978 VW bus and started on a surf trip he had dreamt of for many years: no time limits, no fixed destinations, just 1300 kilometers south from the northern borderline of California towards the border of Mexico. He and his fellow photographer Chris Burkhard would later publish a book called 'The Californian Surf Project' about their journey, but not everything on their trip went smoothly as Soderquist recalls:

"The waves were looking really promising on this early-December day at a break somewhere between San Francisco and Halfmoon Bay. It was freezing cold though – the coldest day since we had started the trip. Anyhow, I wanted to give it a try, but as soon as I hit the water, the pain hit me everywhere: in the head, on my hands and feet, at least as long as I could still feel these parts of my body. 15 minutes later I had enough, I really felt I needed to get out of the water. But it was just then, that the problems started. I was standing in front of my bus and my hands simply didn´t work anymore. **There I was – helpless, soaked, shaking and unable to open the door. There was no other way than asking a complete stranger who just came by to open the door for me.** I then told him how to start the cooker and heat up some water. A few minutes later I was pouring hot water over my wetsuit and already felt a lot better."

So what helps when the swell of the year hits the coast and the temperatures don´t rise above zero?

On warm days, surfers in Iceland wear a 5/3 wetsuit with booties. But when they hit the water during snowfall and temperatures below zero, they put on as much rubber as possible. Nikita's co-founder Runar Omarsson lives on the remote island close to Greenland and knows exactly how to deal with frosty conditions:

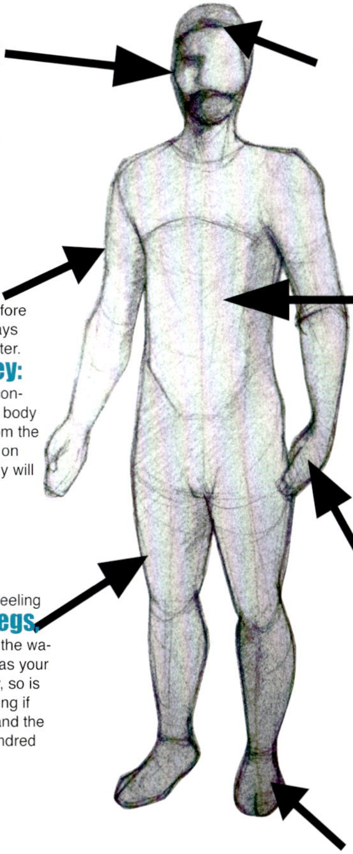

The face is the only body part that is not protected by rubber. Vaseline might help, a trick also used by swimmers crossing the English Channel to protect themselves from the cold for many hours.

Most people underestimate the wind chill. On a day without wind, ten degree water and eight degree air temperature can be quite enjoyable. But if you have a strong wind blowing, it is bitter cold.

Warm yourself up before the session and always move once in the water. **Paddling is key:** If your muscles are constantly working, your body will get heated up from the inside. If you only sit on your board, your body will cool down.

Don´t save on your wetsuit! Most important: It should really fit. **The thickest wetsuit doesn´t work if it's too big.** An attached hood is always better than a separate one. As an additional layer, neoprene rash guards really help a lot.

As soon as you lose feeling in your **arms or legs,** you should get out of the water. At the same time as your feeling is fading away, so is your power – bad timing if your energy is gone and the shore is still a few hundred meters away...

Cold hurts – not immediately, when your hands start to feel thumb, but later, when they start to defrost. This is so painful you could scream out loud. Wearing gloves helps – at least most days.

The feet are a critical part of the body – if they get cold, you start freezing. If 3 mm booties are not warm enough, you should get rigged. If 7 mm don´t work anymore, wear some thin woolen socks in them.

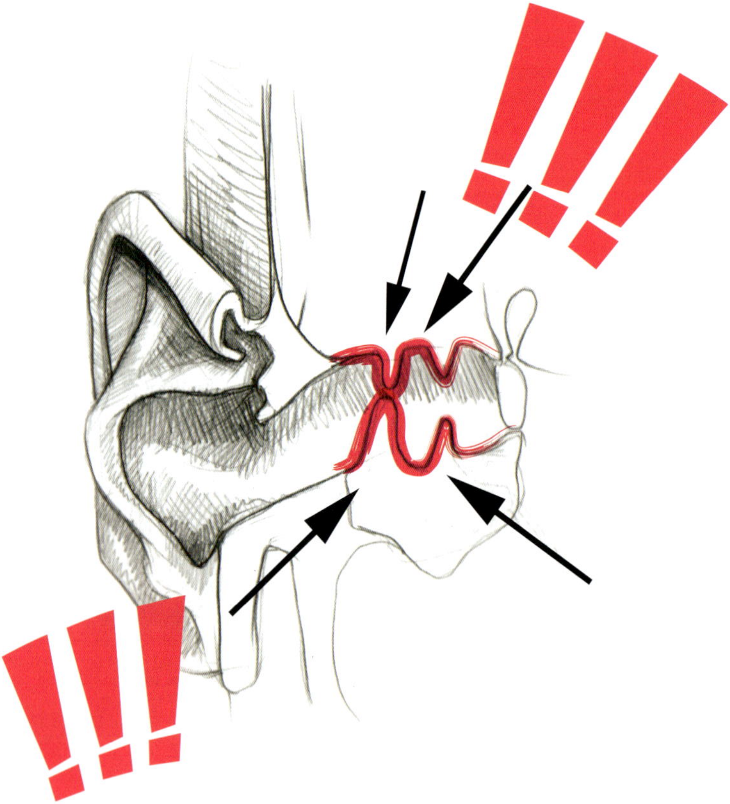

GROWING PAINS

You're in a crowded bar and have to read your friend's lips because you don't understand a word he is saying? You should probably go and see a doctor tomorrow because you might have fallen victim to the dreaded surfer's ear. **It's a sneaky disease that makes the bones of your ear canals grow exuberantly until they look like a stalactite cave or are even completely close up.** **But what can you do against the imminent hearing loss?**

Only surf in the tropics: The main cause for the surfer's ear is the cold that surfers on certain lines of latitude expose themselves to; as a result, the body fights wind chill and ice cold water with the undesirable growth of bones. In the tropics this disease is all but unknown.

Wear earplugs: They prevent water from entering your ear canal and are specifically made for surfers by many companies. When it gets really cold and windy, a neoprene hood additionally helps against the wind chill factor.

Go and see the doctor when you have the feeling that there's still some water stuck in your ears after a session: a typical sign for a surfer's ear. In this case, the doctor probably mills your ear canal open with a driller. There are also stories about particularly serious cases that have to undergo a surgery in which the ears get flapped away from the head and sewed back on.

Don't get old as a surfer: Due to a clinical study conducted in the Spanish Basque Country, the probability to suffer from a surfer's ear rises proportionally to the years you spend with surfing. The results published show that of the participating surfers who are surfing longer than ten years, 86 percent have been diagnosed with an exuberantly growth of bones in their ear canals. Whereas, of the participants surfing less than ten years, only 27 percent were suffering from a surfer's ear.

VICIOUS CYCLE

Rip currents can be your friend and carry you from the beach to the lineup within a few seconds or make your way back through a channel easy. But rip currents can also become your greatest enemy: like when your leash breaks and you try to swim to the shore, but the rip is constantly pushing you away from the beach and carrying you out to the sea – over and over again, until you're finished.

Especially narrow bays pose a threat. Here, rip currents can create a vicious cycle that you need to understand before you are able to escape from it:

1 The lineup: If you lose your board here, you have to swim back to the beach. Don't dive under the breaking waves' white water but instead try to use their power and get carried along with them.

2 The shore: Now you have to be fast and try to get swept right onto the beach with the white water. If you don't make it, you will be punished with another round in the rip current's rotation system. With every wave several tons of water get thrown onto the beach and have to flow off somewhere, in most of the cases back to the open sea.

3 The channel: If you have missed the exit point, you will see the beach disappearing from your sight with every second. Don't try to fight against the rip, you will only waste your energy. Even professional swimmers would lose a duel against a strong rip current: For example, Cesar Cielo holds the world record in the 50 meters freestyle. He crawls the distance in 20.91 seconds, thus making 2.40 meters per second. Currents are often traveling 2.5 to 3 meters per second. Therefore, it's smarter not to fight, but just get yourself carried back into the lineup and give it a new try.

4 From the beach you can easily see how rip currents line up in the bay. Once in the water, you will lose your view. You can easily get back to the beach where the waves break and the white water rolls towards the beach. Where the ocean is darker and the surface seems calm, the water is flowing off from the shore. At these spots you sometimes even see how the sand from the beach gets carried away into the sea.

CUT SCHOOL

The wipeout didn't look very impressive. The surfer was just unlucky that the fin of his surfboard hit his right leg and cut it open. The wound wasn't too deep and only ten centimeters long, no need to get worried. He didn't even think about disinfecting the small cut when he was walking back on the beach of Kuta with a thin line of blood running down his leg.

Months later, he found out that the smallest wounds can be infected by bacteria in tropic waters. Tropical disease specialists advise to even disinfect scratched mosquito bites. But the surfer didn't know about anything like this when he fell asleep in his room with the fan running on maximum power. The next morning was all but enjoyable: "I had fever, a bad headache and a huge bump that looked like a second calf was growing on my shin-bone. The skin surrounding the cut had taken on a dark red color and was stretched to the max. Any movement sent a stabbing pain through the body and my temperature was rising with every hour", recalls the surfer. "I thought about going to the hospital, but my return flight was already scheduled for the next morning; in the end it was only an infection, so why should I be seriously worried? I spent the night in a feverish delirium on a sheet soaked in sweat. On the way to the airport I still felt alright but the flight itself turned into a 20 hour nightmare: Regularly I passed out and found myself in wild fever dreams. The only thing I still know is that my neighbor stole my dinner from my table. During the layover they put me in a wheelchair and rolled me to the next terminal; I noticed the crowds around me like I was in a state of trance. Back home I took a taxi directly to the hospital. For the doctors my infection didn't seem to be a great deal: They identified the bacteria, gave me antibiotics and cut off the rotten mesh around the wound; what was left was a hole as big as a tennis ball. But as soon as the fever had gone, the disaster just began. "There is something wrong with your heart", the doctor said. "The valves don't look too good. It seems like they have been attacked by the bacteria." Probably they went from my leg straight into my heart, now immediate action had to be taken. "Otherwise it could be too late", said the doctor before cutting open my thorax only seven days after the fatal session in Kuta Reef and implanting new heart valves.

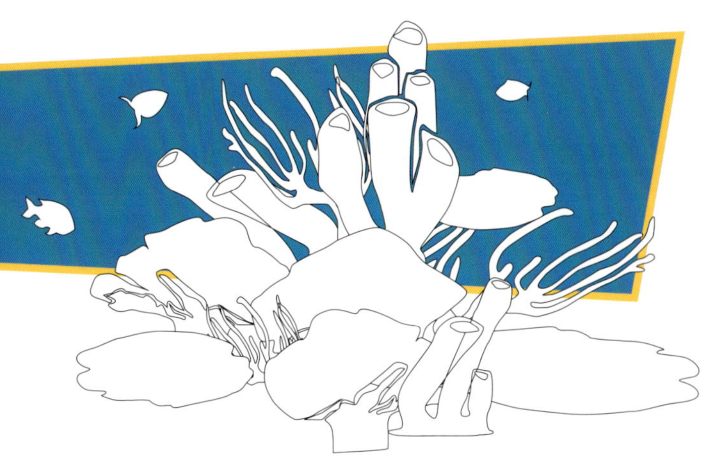

Every surfer will cut themselves on the reef or the fins of their board one day. **The only thing you can do is to take even the smallest injuries seriously, especially in the tropics:** the warmer the water, the greater the risk of an infection.

So what's the best medical practice for coral or fin cuts? First, you need to clean the wound: rinse it with liters of water, you can even scrub it with a new toothbrush to get out all the dirt and sand. Don't shy away from being brutal – if it starts bleeding, foreign particles get flushed out of the wound. Next, you need to disinfect the cut: Tahitian locals use fresh limes and dribble the juice directly into the wound. Most surfers don't travel without betadine, others use Chinese Medicine which any Balinesian pharmacy sells. No matter which of these you are using, take the disinfection serious and don't apply it only once, but as long as the wound is still open. Also, try to keep your arm or leg up to the level of the heart or higher in the first few hours after the accident – swelling, even if you can't see it, can delay healing especially in areas of poor circulation like the shin-bone. But most importantly: When can you go surfing again? Doctors recommend staying out of the water until the wound has fully sealed and healed. But let's face it: If you pay $200 per day on a charter boat, you're probably not going to follow this advice. If the cut is minor and you clean, dry and apply disinfection as well as a new waterproof dressing after every surf, you should be fine.

In case of an infection indicated by red spreading edges or a swelling of the wound, you should immediately see a doctor. Don't hesitate – an infected wound that gets the right medical treatment might ruin a few days of your trip, but an untreated infection can ruin your life!

CRASH TEST DUMMY

Surfing is a form of art – so is the knowledge about how to wipe out properly.

HAWAIIAN PULL OUT

The situation: You are racing down the line, or even surfing deep in the tube, when you see the long wall turning into a massive close out.

The solution: Nothing rivals the elegance of a Hawaiian Pull Out in a situation like this. Just perform a hard turn towards the wall, push your weight forward, grab your outside rail and dive into the wall. If things work out, you surface behind the back of the wave.

RESCUE DIVE

The situation: The waves are small but break hollow over your favorite sandbank. A perfect day to try all the maneuvers that you have been dreaming of for a long time. Your only concern: getting knocked out by your own board.

The solution: A perfect dive. But don't dive in too deep, as you would do when diving off a diving board into a pool – you might directly hit the sandbank. Better hit the surface at a flat angle, like a professional swimmer performing their start dive. Watch out: Don't dive directly in front of your board's nose, rather jump sideways. The wave will do the rest and kick your board out of your way.

STARFISH

The situation: You are surfing on a shallow reef and by no means want to test the sharpness of the corals and rocks underneath the surface.

The solution: Perform the Starfish, even though it will cost you quite an effort. When crashing, most surfers instinctively raise their arms like during a dive; either because they want to protect their head or to escape the breaking lip by plunging into the water. The Starfish works differently: Don't plunge into the water but let yourself fall onto the surface, if possible with your back first. Reach out your arms and legs to the side, like performing a jumping jack. Like this, you won't plunge too deep into the water and will avoid any contact with the reef.

If you are paddling over the reef and towards the channel afterwards and you need to duckdive under a wave, don't take your board by the rails; you wouldn't be the first one to have cut their fingers open... Better put your hands flat onto the board and push it down.

FORWARD ESCAPE

The situation: The swell of the year has arrived and you are surfing one of the biggest waves of your life – unfortunately, things don't work out that well and you know that the worst wipeout of your life is just around the corner.

The solution: Wiping out on big waves is all about minimizing the damage. Golden rule number 1: Try to avoid the breaking lip by all means. If it hits you with full force, it could squeeze all your air out of the lungs. Golden rule number 2: Stay on your board as long as possible and wait until the white water closes in on you; the more distance a broken wave has traveled, the less power it has, meaning: the later the white water swallows you, the less severe your wipeout. Golden rule number 3: Coil yourself up like a ball underwater and protect your face with your hands like a boxer would do – just in case you get washed on a rock. Then, relax and wait until the wave releases you. Don't fight against the water's force, this will only cost you precious oxygen.

ANIMAL WARFARE

Animals are often your best friends, but sometimes they become your worst enemies. For example, when they send you into delirium with one sting. That's exactly what happened to English surfer Daniel Burrows who had a near-death experience thanks to a tiny mosquito.

"The Papeete hostel where I was staying was cramped, dirty and hot under the tin roof. Separating my bunk from a sweating latrine was a thin partition wall that provided little protection from the sound of retching backpackers and mosquitoes that rose in clouds from its swampy mess as night fell. It was a breading ground of insect borne disease. Dosed with beer I spent sleepless nights mummified in a sweat soaked sheet as protection against the droning waves of bloodthirsty mosquitos. I cut out after a week to camp closer to the water at the waist of the island. The waves were pumping and sleeping in my tent was luxury compared to the hell of the hostel. This was the Tahiti I had imagined. After only a couple of days, I was consumed by fever, my head thumping. At first I thought I was dehydrated from the sun and surf and chilled in the shade, but the fever didn't abate. By the next morning I was unable to walk and lay in my sleeping bag as the sun beat down on my tent. It was over 100 degrees but I was shivering, sweating, vomiting and unable to eat. Five days in I woke with my limbs the color of eggplant and my joints had ceased. Fighting back feverish hallucinations I packed my wallet, passport and medical kit into my daypack and crawled to the roadside hoping that someone would stop and help. Thankfully, a local guy pulled over, slung me in the back of his pickup and dropped me at the French military hospital. Drifting in and out of consciousness all I remember were the lights of a spotless intensive care unit and beautiful nurses. Apparently, I was a day from death when I arrived at the hospital, with advanced dengue, a secondary blood infection and water on the lungs. When I returned to my tent two weeks later I found that someone had stolen my clothes. Thankfully my board was still there, but it would be a month before I was strong enough to surf again."

Mosquitos can knock you out with dengue fever or malaria, other animals use poison to paralyze your muscles or cut through your skin with their teeth like a hot knife through butter.

Beastly enemies lurk everywhere, never let down your guard...

VAMPIRE SLAYER

The Anopheles mosquito is no bigger than a 5 cent coin but the world's most dangerous animal. It transmits the tropical disease malaria, which kills more than one million people every year. The following section tells you how you can protect yourself against these tiny bloodsuckers even in the most remote corner of Indonesia.*

Malaria prophylaxis

The heaviest weapon against the disease. You must take the anti-malaria drugs before your departure and even several weeks after your return. However, as a result, the reproduction of malaria agents in human blood will be prevented in the case of an infection. A prophylaxis is only recommended for short stays of up to four weeks (the corresponding drugs shouldn't be taken for a longer period of time) in areas with high risk of malaria such as Lombok, Madagascar or the Solomon Islands. Some substances in the drugs might constrain your spatial perception and are not really recommended for a surf trip. However, there are different medications with varying side effects and you should tell your doctor that you are an athlete.

Stand-by treatment

In this case, you carry an emergency medication with you that is only used when suffering from conspicuous symptoms (eg. sudden high fever that occurs earliest one week after the arrival) and kills the malaria agents in the blood. Recommended for longer stays (longer than four weeks) and in areas with low or moderate risk of malaria.

Mosquito repellent spray

Products with chemical substances like DEET (Diethyloluamid) or Icaridin work best, but they also irritate the skin and can damage your nervous system. Well-tolerated alternatives are insect repellents based on natural ingredients like eucalyptus, tea-tree or cedar oil. In rare cases mosquitos might find their way out to the lineup or on a boat – if you want to play it safe, buy waterproof sunscreen with insect repellent.

Air condition

Mosquitos hate the cold! Therefore, you are relatively safe in a hotel room with AC. If your room only has a fan, turn it on the highest level – similar to low temperatures, mosquitos don't like wind.

Mosquito net

Anyone who is on a budget trip and doesn't sleep in a room with AC shouldn't travel without one. According to the World Health Organization (WHO), mosquito nets should be insecticide-treated and have a net mesh size of 2 millimeters – this guarantees perfect air circulation and at the same time mosquitos don't have any chance.

Plug-In Mosquito Killer

We were a bit sceptic, but our expert swears by these plug-ins! The devices generate an ultrasonic sound that equals the sound of a flying male mosquito. The result: Female mosquitos, exclusively transmitting malaria, take a flight. Place the plug-in close to the door or a window – this will keep the mosquitos out of the room.

Garlic

Indo expert and pro surfer Timmy Turner swears by this household remedy: "It will make your blood taste like rubbish to mosquitos. The only disadvantage: Your friends will forgo you!" Tropical doctors don't trust this natural mosquito protection, they say: what helps against one mosquito, might have no effect at all on another.

*Tropical doctor Susanne Pechel shared her expert knowledge with us. On the following pages she also explains the real dangers of malaria.

How dangerous is malaria?

Tropical doctor Susanne Pechel knows what happens to your body in case of a malaria infection and which other tropical disease can be a threat.

"What most people don't know: Malaria starts in the liver. When you get bitten by an infected mosquito, it only takes 30 seconds until the germ attacks the organ. It reproduces itself in the liver cells until they burst and thousands of merozoites, a kind of micro parasite, get flushed into the bloodstream. The same now happens to the red blood cells: They get infested by the micro parasites and burst. At this point, approximately one week after the bite, the first symptoms of the disease set in: fever, shivering, headache and back pain.

It is very hard to distinguish malaria from a flu. Basically, you should follow this advice: Any fever in an area with malaria risk is suspicious and you should go and see a doctor as soon as possible – nobody else can make a reliable diagnosis and either tell you it's all fine or treat you with the right medication. Rapid tests that you can take with you on the trip might be handy but the smallest mistake in their handling can lead to wrong results. This could end in a disaster if you are infected with malaria tropica: Without a treatment, every fifth person infected with this form of malaria dies. The reason: The infested blood cells clump together, get stuck at the vascular wall and constrain the blood flow. Cramps, neurological disorders and coma are the result. Often the germs also infest other organs which can cause swellings of the liver and spleen as well as pulmonary edema and acute renal failure. Malaria tropica is the most dangerous and at the same time the most widespread form of malaria: It can be found in almost all areas with a malaria risk and is responsible for more than 70 percent of all malaria infections.

Far less widespread and dangerous are the two other forms of malaria. While 80 percent of the red blood cells get infested when suffering from malaria tropica, only 1 percent are affected in case of malaria tertiana and malaria quartana. The course of disease is not as severe – every three respectively four days you will get struck by heavy fever but in most cases the infection will process without complications. However, both forms of malaria can break out again after months or even years as germs sometimes remain in the liver cells and get reactivated after a 'rest period'.

90 percent of all malaria infections occur in Africa, particularly the west coast is blamed as one of the most dangerous high-risk areas. Worldwide there is a differentiation between areas with a low, moderate and high risk of malaria, but sometimes only a few kilometers can make a difference. For example, Bali is an area with a low risk of malaria, while Lombok, which is only a few hours away, is a high-risk area. Generally speaking the risk of an infection is higher during the raining season when mosquitos have a great choice of breeding grounds like puddles and ponds to lay their eggs. Therefore, not only the mosquito population but also the risk of an infection grows abruptly. Where and when you have to expect a risk of malaria, you can very easily find out on www.fitfortravel.nhs.uk.

The Anopheles mosquito mainly bites during dawn and in the night, but during daytime you have to face other dangers; for example, the Asian tiger mosquito which transmits dengue fever. This tropical disease mainly occurs in South and South East Asia, particularly in Thailand and Indonesia. Dengue fever is also known as breakbone fever because besides fever the symptoms also include muscle and joint pain. **An infection gives you lifelong immunity but only against the virus type you got infected with.** If you get infected a second time and with another virus type, the disease might develop into the life-threatening dengue hemorrhagic fever, resulting in internal bleedings and death in five percent of all cases. While you can protect yourself against malaria with various medications, there is only one cure for dengue fever: Don't get bitten!"

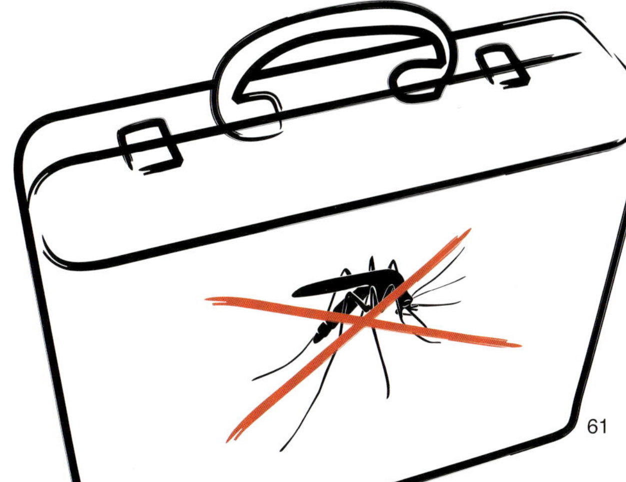

JAWS TRACKING

An average of 64 shark attacks occur each year, five of which are fatal. The risk to fall victim is 1 to 165 million, lower odds than picking six winning lottery numbers plus a bonus number (1 to 140 million). But some spots are more dangerous than others.

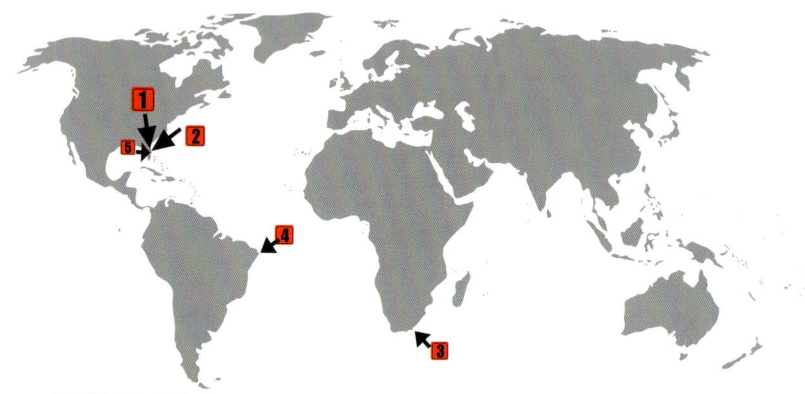

TOP 5

The world's five most **dangerous** surf spots, nowhere have more surfers been attacked since 1845. Surprisingly, Australia and California don't show up in the statistic.

1 New Smyrna Beach/ Florida: The front-runner of the attack stats: 98 attacks, none fatal. Here, the widely-spread blacktip sharks don't get bigger than 1.50 meters and in most cases their bites are not life-endangering.

2 Ponce Inlet/ Florida: Located only 23 kilometers north from New Smyrna Beach. 24 attacks on surfers, none fatal.

3 Nahoon Reef/ South Africa: One attack almost every year. Great whites or bull sharks are responsible for most of the 15 attacks on surfers, one was fatal.

4 Boa Viagem/ Brazil: After 12 attacks on surfers, one in which was fatal, the government made surfing illegal on this stretch of coast in 1995; the law is still enforced.

5 Jupiter Beach Inlet/ Florida: Ten attacks on surfers, none fatal.

THE STATS

Since 1580, 2463* shark attacks have been counted, 471 were fatal. The ranking of the countries most popular for sharks:

Florida	*637/ 11	Puerto Rico	10/ 2
South Africa	230/ 49	Indonesia	6/ 2
New South Wales/ Au	186/ 56	Ecuador	6/ 0
Queensland/ Au	158/ 47	Venezuela	4/ 2
Hawaii	105/ 8	France	4/ 1
California	104/ 9	Costa Rica	4/ 1
Brazil	90/ 21	Argentina	4/ 0
Western Australia/ Au	59/ 13	Dominican Republic	3/ 2
Mexico	38/ 19	Madagascar	3/ 1
South Australia/ Au	35/ 15	French Polynesia	3/ 1
Victoria / Au	30/ 8	Spain	3/ 0
New Zealand/ South Island	23/ 4	Sri Lanka	3/ 0
Fiji	22/ 8	El Salvador	2/ 1
New Zealand/ North Island	17/ 4	Great Britain	2/ 0
Japan	12/ 8	Nicaragua	2/ 0
Tasmania / Au	12/ 4	Canary Islands	2/ 0
Philippines	11/ 6	Cape Verde	1/ 1
Mozambique	11/ 3	Israel	1/ 0
Panama	10/ 5	Martinique	1/ 0
Italy	10/ 2	Senegal	1/ 0

* Last updated: January 30, 2012   *attacks / deaths

THE PREDATORS

Worldwide about 500 species of sharks are known and more than 50 have already attacked humans. The greatest danger comes from the notorious "big three", they are responsible for half of all attacks: tiger shark, bull shark and the great white. The latter have already left a trace of horror as they are credited with every third attack, and not even small boats offer protection from this predator. In 1936, a great white jumped on a fish trawler off the coast of South Africa and dragged a crew member into the ocean. During an attack, a human has almost no chance against these animals: **A six meter long great white weighs more than a ton,** their jaws have a bite force of 1.8 tons and they can chunk off 14 kilos of meat from their prey with only one bite.

PREVENTION TRAINING

Volusia County, on the Atlantic coast of Florida, is not only known for its long stretch of beaches or the NASCAR races of Daytona, but also holds the record for the most shark attacks on the planet. Within the last decade, 21 percent of all shark attacks worldwide happened along the 75 kilometer long shore of Volusia. Statistically, it is very easy to avoid an encounter with one of the swimming predators: Don't go bathing in the ocean on Sundays, don't swim in a water depth of more than two meters and avoid wearing black-and-white shorts or bathing suits. These factors have applied to most of the victims. Unfortunately, real life is not always so simple: Sharks are not weekend warriors and attack more often on the weekends. It's the mass of people that go to the beach on Sundays that increase the chances of an encounter with a shark. The same goes for the water depth: **It's not more risky to swim in a depth of 1.5 meters than 2 meters** – most swimmers simply don't dare to swim out that far. After all, the statistics don't explain when and where sharks are more likely to attack, but only when and where the biggest crowds can be found and what kind of bathing suit fashion is up to date.

Nevertheless, surfers can minimize the risk to find themselves in the jaws of a shark by following some simple advice:

Sharks are very picky in choosing their hunting grounds and it is recommended to **avoid spots where attacks have already occurred.** Let's have a closer look at an example in California: The beach of Ano Nuevo next to Santa Cruz is located at the southern boundary of the infamous Red Triangle which is known for its high population of great whites. There are surfers in the water when there are waves, but not one of them has been attacked so far. It seems like there are no sharks at all in this area. This impression is wrong. If you walk towards the end of the cliff which reaches out to the ocean at the northern end of the beach, you will most likely see a great white within one or two hours. The sharks are there but nothing draws them to the lineup.

However, most of the time things are different because the best waves often break exactly where sharks hunt – close to river mouths, on reef edges or at point breaks in front of land tongues that steeply fall off into the ocean. Those who surf here inevitably enter shark grounds. Nevertheless, the risk of an attack can be reduced if you consider factors such as the time of day: American shark experts call sunrise and sunset "killer times". **Also avoid certain seasons, for example, the "sardine runs" between May and July on South Africa's east coast.** Then, millions of sardines swim north and put the predators off the coast in a literal feeding frenzy. The same happens during the "mullet runs" between September and October off the American east coast of Florida and Georgia when swarms of red mullets move towards the south and attract sharks. Rainfall can also intensify the risk by raising river levels and washing garbage and carcasses into the ocean and causing the water to turn murky.

Apart from environmental factors, surfers should keep a close eye on what's happening around them. **A fisherman dumps garbage and by-catch over board within your range of sight? You better paddle straight to the beach.** You see a seal bitten in half lying on the beach? Maybe it's not the best idea to go for a session at this break. And if you sit in the lineup watching a seal swimming for its life, you should think about what could have terrified the animal.

FIN SCIENCE

The tip makes the difference

A fin rising from the water is enough to make your blood curdle. But a second glance might unmask the presumed shark as a dolphin.

The dorsal fin of a **dolphin** is bent backwards like the rear end of an old Cadillac.

A **shark** fin is formed more like a triangle with straight lines.

SHARK SCHOOL

 You are circled by a shark. What to do? Behavior scientist and shark expert Doctor Erich Ritter knows how you can send a shark swimming.

1. Stop any activity! If you're paddling away, the shark might get interested in you and see you as a potential prey. Slowly glide off your surfboard, put your arms on the top of the deck and let your legs hang loose without making any movement. Such a vertical position seems abnormal to a shark and makes it more cautious – hardly any sea dweller swims in a stand up position.

2. Always face the shark! If he circles you, cautiously pivot with your surfboard – but only slightly move your arms and never your legs.

3. Guide the shark! If he swims towards you and is in touchable distance, you should guide the shark by touching its snout or top of the head area. If it's necessary to have a more forceful response, it is okay to push a shark as long as you don't hit the animal.

4. Become a predator! If the shark keeps coming back for a few times and you feel threatened, you should move towards the shark. Sharks are not use to being approached. Such a move suggests another top predator, which will irritate the shark – it will back off.

5. Know its weak point! Whenever sharks try to hurt or kill each other, they "go for" the gills. You don't have to go that far: In case a shark attacks you, it often suffices to touch its gills with your flat hand and the animal will back off. Why? Sharks react to signals they know, also if they don't know who or what might be the trigger. Unknown signals like hits or kicks are rarely successful as it is mere luck when the shark surceases from you.

Note: There are no dangerous sharks, only dangerous situations – if you react correspondingly, you can avoid the worst-case scenario!

LITTLE PRICKS

They lurk in the sand and in crevices and silently sneak up on you under water – only to spoil your day.

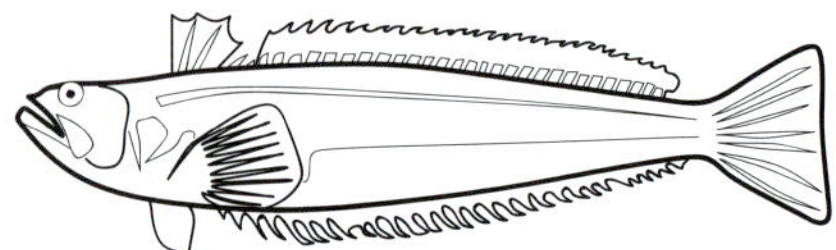

Weever fish

What: A fish with a length of 15 to 50 centimeters that loves to burry itself under the sand only a few meters from the shore. If you step on one, it piles the poisonous stings on its back into your foot.

Where: In the North Sea, in the Mediterranean Sea and on any Atlantic coast in Europe – from Norway to Portugal.

How: At first, it' s not that bad. It takes a few minutes until it starts hurting. The best remedy: Water that is so hot you can barely stand it. The heat breaks up the poisons' structure and makes it ineffective. Some surfers say it is sufficient to scuffling your feet when walking in shallow water. In doing so, the fish are startled and escape before you step on them.

Jellyfish

What: Jelly-like creatures that consist of 99 percent water and terrify with their long tentacles equipped with poisonous capsules. The slightest contact is enough – they will immediately shoot their poison into the skin of the victim.

Where: Everywhere, but not all species are equally dangerous. In Australia and the Pacific around the Philippines the box jellyfish cause a lot of trouble and casualties. In Europe you should watch out for the Portuguese man-of-war, which can be responsible for painful incinerations. Luckily they are easy to spot due to their purple-blue balloon that drifts on the surface.

How: The pain is somewhere between a whiplash and a hot iron pole hitting your skin. First, you should try to remove the rest of the tentacles including their poison. Never use tap water because this will cause even more poisonous capsules to explode. Just rinse the affected skin parts with salt water. Lifeguards spray shaving foam onto the skin and scrape it off with a credit card or something similar. You can have the same effect with wet sand that you place on your skin: let it dry and then scrape it off. Vinegar might help as well, but this is a double-edged sword as it only helps for a few species. For example, the box jellyfish – when you do the same after being attacked by a Portuguese man-of-war, vinegar only makes it worse.

Sea urchin

What: Most of them only have a diameter of a few centimeters but are equipped with numerous spines. If you step on an urchin, a few broken off spines will definitely get stuck in your foot. Not even boots offer 100 percent protection as the spines will find their way through the soft rubber sole. Some species in the Caribbean Sea even defend themselves with thin, 30 centimeters long XXL spines.

Where: Everywhere, from New Zealand to Portugal to Hawaii. Sometimes urchins flock together in colonies and it appears as if entire boulders are covered by a stingy carpet.

How: Try to remove the spines the same day. First, you need to soak the affected parts of your body in warm water. When the skin looks wrinkled and has become soft, you can try to get the spines out with a needle and a tweezer – just as if you would pull out a small splinter of wood. Unfortunately, the spines are extremely fragile and break easily. When you notice that you can't remove them, rather wait before cutting your whole foot open. Normally, the body takes care of foreign material and either disperses the parts of the spines within two weeks or slowly lifts them up to the surface of the skin. Don't forget to disinfect your wound to prevent tiny but deep cuts from becoming inflamed.

PS: Urine is a magic bullet! Just pee on the puncture or the incineration and everything will be fine – this is at least what Spanish fishermen and Australian surfers say to do. There is no scientific proof for this procedure, but you never know...

FEMALE ISSUES

"When men surf, it's that ape nature", says Australian pro surfer Layne Beachley while making a Tarzan call. "It's all about competing and showing your ego, and often an aggressive vibe is dominating the line-up." According to Layne, that changes with girls in the water. "It produces a calmness, because we can laugh at ourselves. It's not about who is surfing the most waves, but about having a good time out there. This positive vibe automatically transfers to the guys." Unfortunately, women are still an exception in the lineups, the statistics count one female surfer per ten male surfers. It's a bit like entering a bar by yourself that is full of men. All of a sudden all eyes are on you. You feel uncomfortable and make mistakes that you normally would avoid. "Girls often feel intimidated by men in the lineup, and being timid is what's going to hold you back in every aspect of surfing", says Layne who ended her professional surf career in 2008 and is nowadays organizing girls-only surf classes. Therefore, her best advice against male dominance in the lineup: girl power – "the more women in the water, the better!"

Too much testosterone can ruin your session. The same goes for a bikini that exposes more than you hoped for. Hazards that men don't have to fear also wait for you on land: for example, dates that turn into a pyscho killer or love-stricken locals that don't accept your denial.

It's not always easy to be a surfer girl, but some tricks might help.

PERFORMANCE TRAINING

Layne Beachley has won seven world titles, but as a teenager she didn't have an easy time. Often she was the only girl in the lineup and had to take a lot of insults and bullying from the guys. This only made her stronger: "I knew I had as much right to the ocean as the guys did so I learned to stand up for myself." Still today, the 40 year old Australian hasn't forgotten how hard it can be for the girls to get their fair share of waves in a male dominated lineup and shares some of her tricks.

Don't compare apples and oranges!

I always remind my friends that I was a beginner once, too. I caught so much crap from the guys in the water for being a girl out there. It was back in the day when it really wasn't acceptable for girls to be in the water. I know I used to put myself down before anyone else had a chance to. I was hurting myself instantly in order to prevent someone else from doing it. It gets to a point where you feel like you're not good enough. But then you ask yourself: who are you not good enough for? There's no point in comparing yourself to other people. You are good enough if you want to be. 80 percent of surfing happens in your head – if you think you fall, you will fall, and if you keep telling yourself you are not good enough, your session certainly is going to be crap.

Respect yes! Intimidation no!

Everyone feels intimidated by surfers who are better than they are, and it's not just the girls. Imagine how I felt in the Mentawais sitting in the lineup with Occy, Shane Beschen and Sunny Garcia! But then I noticed that there were times they would take a spot down the line when they weren't feeling good enough, too. It's the same thing when I'm freesurfing with guys who aren't as good as I am – they get intimidated by me. It's just that pecking order thing, and it's something you'll have to face with surfing no matter what level you're at.

If you can't beat 'em, don't join them!

Most good waves are going to have a thick crowd. Unless your skills and confidence are as high as the majority of guys out there, you're not going to get a wave. If you feel like you should sit inside with the grommets, then that's what you should do. Or, go off and surf waves that are of lesser value until you get your confidence up and ability so that you're comfortable enough to get in there and fight for your fair share of waves. If you keep putting yourself in a situation where you're too timid to be catching waves, you're not going to progress.

You need the skills to pay the bills!

Ultimately, you have to have the confidence to go. If you don't, whether you're good enough or not, you shouldn't be out there. Especially when you're learning, it's best to find a wave that's not so crowded, or to go out with friends so you're not embarrassed wiping out and don't feel bad about not being good. Stick to surfing where you're more comfortable and stay there until you know you're ready to step up.

DRESS CODES

Your first trip to the tropics and you can't hardly wait to go surfing in a bikini. Highly motivated, you paddle towards the lineup and duckdive a set of big waves. Suddenly, you feel there is something wrong. The waves have stolen the little pieces of fabric off your body and you try to get your naked body back to the shore without being seen. An embarrassing situation that can be easily avoided with the right bikini...

The perfect bikini top looks like a sports bra: the straps are crossed on the back and nothing gets out of place. This cut is called Racerback, ideally the straps are adjustable.

Also a good choice: fixed halter neck or bandeau tops that can be tied at the neck and on the back. Look for large straps – they don't get out of place that easily, can be tightened really strong and the fabric barely wears out.

The tighter, the better – your panties should stay in place even after the heaviest wipeout! Most pro surfers go for short hipster pants that sit low on your hips. Tip: Buy them a size smaller because they will wear out in the water.

It's not always about color! Bright or neon colors might seem alluring, but keep in mind that they will soon get bleached out by the saltwater and sun. Pastel or light colors last longer.

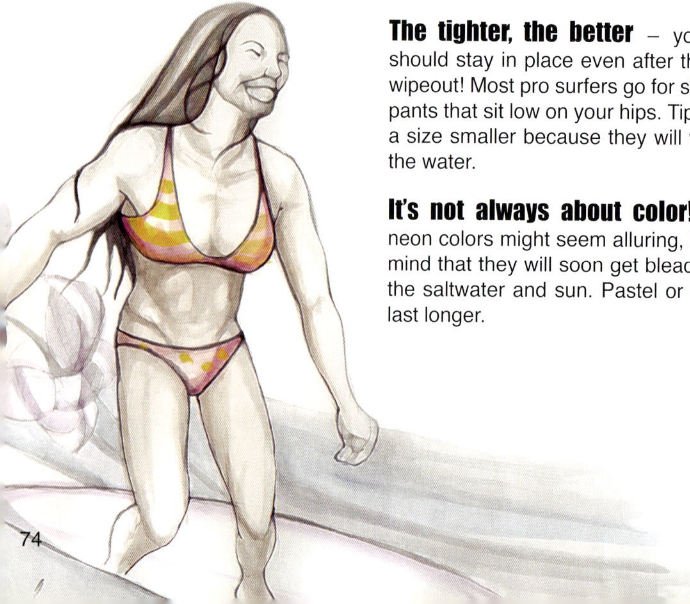

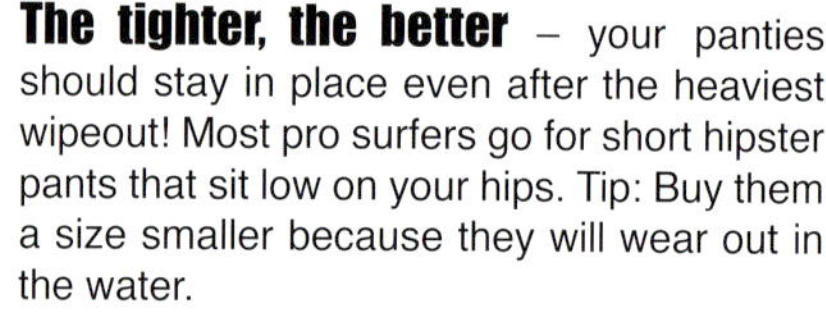

BAD BIKINI

Keep your hands off Brazilian bikinis!
The triangle tops are loosely held together by ties and will get out of place with every paddle stroke. The pants are even worse: The thin side-ties wear out really fast – after the fifth session the bottom will give in and slip down.

No plastic closures!
They easily erode in the saltwater and break. The result: You are sitting topless in the lineup.

Avoid bikini tops with pads:
They might provide an impressing décolleté at the beach, but will get out of place after the first duckdive and look like misplaced socks.

Boy shorts might look handy, but they are not:
the more fabric, the more water can get in and the bottom will get out of place.

KILLER INSTINCT

According to the FBI, between 200 and 400 serial killers are on the loose in the United States alone. They secretly live among us and wait for their next victim. If you are at the wrong place at the wrong time, you could run into one in a dodgy bar in the middle of nowhere.

CRIMINAL PROFILE

Eight red flags* that you should watch out for on a date to recognize a serial killer:

He's an American. 76% of all serial homicides happen in the United States.

Statistically, most killers are between 20 and 30 years old.

Dark circles around his eyes? Half of killers suffer from sleeping problems.

He is a local. Most of the time, serial killers strike close to their home – they feel safer in familiar surroundings.

Is he playing with matches throughout your date? Almost one third of all perpetrators have committed arson.

He smiles while kicking a stray cat under the table. 46% of all serial killers tortured animals as teenagers, 36% continue this behavior after adolescence.

He doesn't like to talk about his past. Most serial killers don't remember their childhood in a positive way. Often crime and alcohol were involved, in 47% of the cases the father had left the family before they turned 12.

You have never seen him before. Serial killers choose their victims randomly, in most cases they kill strangers.

* From a FBI study about serial killers

PREY PATTERN
You should be even more careful when the following criteria* apply. They make you the perfect victim:

You are female (82% of all victims are women)

Age: Between 23 and 29 years old

Relationship status: Single (80% of all victims are not married)

You are traveling alone. 63% of all victims do not have an escort on their trip

Small and petite? Almost one third of all victims are physically inferior to the perpetrator

Shy and insecure? Serial killers look for victims they don't expect to be fierce and put up a good fight. Self-confident women are less likely to fall victim

You are helping out someone whose car broke down or you enter the car of a stranger. A vehicle is involved in 85% of all serial homicides

RESCUE PLAN
All of the precautions haven't helped: The nice guy turns into a psycho and has trapped you. And now? Criminal expert Stephan Harbort knows what to do:

Get him involved in a conversation! If you manage to build up a personal relationship with the killer, you are not an anonymous, passive victim anymore – this might disturb his violent fantasies and alter his plan to kill you.

Surprise him! Often perpetrators act according to a pre-rehearsed play – he already has all of the scenes memorized. When the victim doesn't act as expected, it alienates the killer and he escapes. For example, a German serial killer let a few women go because they didn't defend themselves as he had imagined it in his violent fantasies, but instead offered to kiss him.

Defend yourself! If nothing helps, the fight is your last chance. Resistance might cause the killer to abandon his plans and escape. But be careful: This only works out when you defend yourself with everything you got – halfhearted attempts always end deadly.

Liz Clark should know – the 31-year old surfer has already seen more places in her present life than most of us will ever do. In 2006 she set off to sail from her home in California into the unknown. Her only goal: to discover foreign shores and surf virgin breaks. Since then she has been to Guatemala, Costa Rica, Panama, the Galapagos Islands, the Tuamotu Atolls, Line Islands in the Republic of Kiribati and Tahiti to name just a few, and her trip is not over yet.

"I guess nature and humans are potentially equally dangerous, but I have had far fewer dangerous encounters with humans than with natural forces. For example: **I've been caught in multiple horrific lightning storms that I hope never to relive**. When I encounter lightning at sea, I can try to steer around the worst of it, but often it's virtually impossible to avoid. The mast of my boat is like a giant lightning rod in the middle of the ocean, so it's terrifying being near lightning as it can fry all your electronics or potentially sink the boat by blowing a hole in the hull. Once a bolt struck so close in the night that I saw the light spectrum and a huge splash where it hit the water. On another occasion when I was freediving to untangle my anchor chain from some coral, five gray sharks swam over me from above and I had to wait on the bottom until they passed before surfacing. One rather traumatizing moment was also getting caught inside at Teahupoo.

My general approach is to take things one little step at a time and try to always prepare for the worst. I really fear only lightning and hurricanes. But in this lifestyle, you can never really let your guard down. I must be constantly vigilant even when the boat is at anchor in order to assure its and my security. It can be quite tiring.

There are certainly places that are more dangerous to travel whether you are male or female. It is always important, especially for girls, to do your research before going to another country to find out what the current situation is with the government, and what is culturally acceptable to wear, do or say. In my experience, if you **respect the local culture of a place**, you are unlikely to have problems. And I almost always cover myself up with longer shorts and shirts, tie my hair back, and make an effort not to overtly attract attention to myself. All the countries I have visited have been safe enough for girls to travel alone as long as they are wary and respectful.

In some countries it might get a bit annoying when being asked questions like "You wanna marry me?" or "Where is your husband?" by men all the time. I usually completely ignore them or act nice but oblivious, and make my way as quickly as possible away from them without causing a scene. If someone is really persistent and I start to feel threatened, I'm immediately assertive, tell them to 'back off', and try to make my way close to other people. **It is important to be able to read people well**. I generally try to spot 'good' people and make friends with them as soon as I get to a new place, that way I have network of people watching out for me.

If I surf a shallow reef alone, I often snorkel the reef to get to know what's down there. And most of all, I find it's important to know and respect my limits. I don't push them too far in this kind of situation. I often start by sitting on the shoulder, getting to know the character of the wave first, and then making my way deeper toward the bowl as I gain confidence.

While traveling there will always be situations that you don't expect – hold-ups, transportation cancellations, or changes in the way you 'thought' things would go. At the beginning of my trip, I would get frustrated when equipment broke down or the weather didn't accommodate my chosen destination. I eventually learned to go with the flow, be patient, and find the positive side of these situations. Once I let go of trying to control the way things went, new worlds of learning and unexpected opportunities opened up to me. In my experience, it is always better to accept each situation for what it is and try to work with it, not against it. A positive attitude makes all the difference in enjoying yourself or being miserable. An unexpected twist in your trip can often lead to something even better than you had planned!

**And one last advice:
Always trust your instinct
– live by it."**

Liz Clark

UNPLEASANT SURPRISES

One moment you are feeling like heaven on earth, but in the next second you are staring into the abyss. This is what happened to Australian pro surfer Dean Morrison on a fishing trip in 2008: Everything started fun when Dean and four of his mates left towards Hamilton Island, twelve kilometers off the coast. One of the five was running the boat on full throttle while the rest piled down the tail-end to avoid the spray that was being whipped up by the boat as it bounced flat-chat across the sea. For a real laugh, the "captain" spontaneously down throttled to zero – bad idea! The wake overtook the boat, flooded it, and it sank within ten seconds. "We were still holding our beer cans when the boat just gave away underneath us", says Dean. "Our only hope was an island a few kilometers away that we could hardly spot anymore due to the fading light." Hours later, the five friends were still swimming for land. "It was pitch-black, you couldn't see anything", Dean recalls. "But all of a sudden I hit something under water – rocks!" Somehow he had found the island without seeing it. But to the friends' dismay, the situation didn't really improve from here. Dressed only in their boardshorts, the boys spent the night huddling together for warmth only to find out the next morning that the only inhabitants of the island were big, venomous black snakes. They didn't see any other solution than swimming to the next island, which was approximately 15 kilometers away – an almost insurmountable challenge given their devitalized, dehydrated condition. To top it off, what they did not know was that this stretch of water was infested with big crocs, tiger sharks and deadly box jellyfish. Somehow, they avoided all these predators and when they finally got picked up by a couple in a boat after endless hours, they could not say much more than: "Please get us out of here!"

But not only snakes, crocs or sharks can cause trouble. Sometimes it's a ding in your board, being seasick for days or the loss of all your travel budget at the end of the world.

Unpleasant surprises always come out of the blue so watch out!

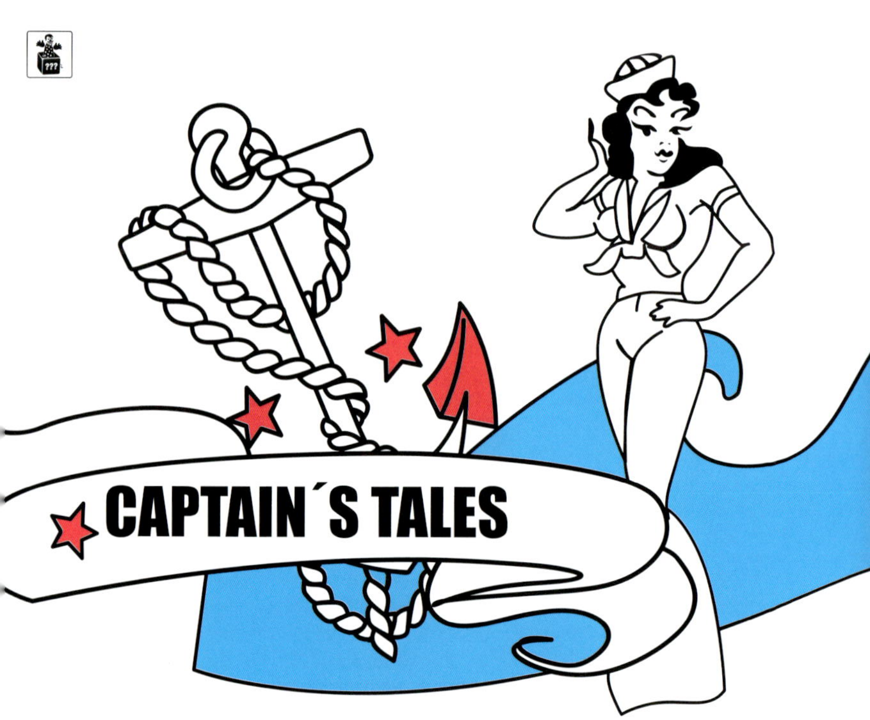

For years now, skipper Klaus Baumgartner has been cruising around Indonesia with his sail boat, taking his guests from one surf break to the next and giving them the trip of their lifetime. But he also knows what kind of trouble can ruin your trip and how to avoid it.

Sea sickness: Can get you down and hits almost everyone. Depending on the sea condition and your sensitivity, you might end up on the railing, unable to stand up without instantly vomiting again. The best remedy: pills against sea sickness, they are a magic bullet. But don't wait until you become sick and then take the pills. At this point it's already too late and the pill will exit your stomach before your body can absorb the curing substances. There are also spots on the boat where you feel less motion and are less prone to becoming sea sick. Basically, you can follow this rule: The closer you are to the bow or to the rear end and the higher you are on the boat, the more you will feel the motion of the sea. Therefore, the best spot is as deep as possible and exactly in the middle of the boat. A small consolation for you: After the first days on board, the worst is over. The human body is very good at adjusting to difficult situations and will get use to the shaky ground pretty fast.

Board fever: Are not very common on a boat trip as it's easy to make surfers happy. If there are waves, everyone is stoked. In addition to this, give them something to eat and all is right with the world. When it's flat, some frustration might set in, but it's more likely that the mood is going to change to the worst on one of these sailing trips in the Mediterranean Sea: These people only sail, drink, sleep and don't do much else – after a week on board in the tightest of quarters, you know whose your friend and whose your enemy.

Injuries: Should absolutely be avoided. On a boat trip in Indo, help is far. It takes days when you're off the coast of Timor and in need of a doctor. And then you most likely end up in a jungle hospital where I personally wouldn't like to get treated. So watch out a bit, but small reef cuts are not too bad. You're more likely to catch an infection in the dirty streets of Bali, in comparison to that, a boat is clinically clean.

Nightmares: Can quickly become reality in Indo. A few years ago, a group of divers had been carried away by the current and the boat was unable to locate them. Fortunately, they could swim to a deserted island. The bad news: The island was infested by Komodo dragons, huge lizards that also eat humans. The divers had to defend themselves for two days by throwing stones at the beasts before they were rescued. In Indo, raw wilderness can still be found which is totally different to the lives most of us know. Another nightmare is going over board at night because you didn't hold on to the railing while peeing. If you're in a situation like this, yell as loud as you can because if nobody hears you, it's over.

SINKING SHIP

It happened out of the blue and in the middle of the night. In October 2010, two surf charter boats anchored next to the spot Macaronis in the Mentawais. Suddenly, the Australian skipper of one of the boats heard a rumbling sound which grew louder and louder – like a jumbo jet approaching the landing. Then he saw the huge white water ball wallowing into the protected bay, sweeping the other charter boat away and dashing it into his own boat. In the moment of the impact a huge explosion could be heard from the lower deck. "Everything happened within seconds and all of a sudden my boat was on fire", the captain recalls. Immediately he called everyone on deck, advised them to throw everything that might float into the water and jump off the boat. There was not much more the skipper could do. Luckily, all surfers and the entire crew of the two boats could save their skin, swim to shore and escape the three meter high tsunami that hit the Mentawais.

A story that demonstrates how easy a boat trip can turn into a battle for survival. But what to do when you are in deep water in your cabin?

Don't just jump over the railing without giving it a second thought!
It's worth taking a few seconds to throw a life raft over board or to grab a life vest. Even a surfboard is better than nothing – when you have to stay over water without anything floating, you will soon lose your energy and drown. Bad timing if you first need to search your life vest while the water climbs up – better check this out when entering the boat for the first time.

A life raft is probably the best place to be after the loss of the boat.
There are many stories told by survivors who were floating on the ocean for months before they were rescued. If you are not lucky and get found, your only chance is to get washed ashore by a current. But you can influence this situation: Most life rafts have a drift anchor that stabilizes the boat during heavy sea. But when it's flat it throttles the speed of the life raft in the current. The slower you move across the ocean the more time it will take until you reach land. Therefore, it is best to reel in the drift anchor when the weather situation is stable.

Having no food is not the biggest problem of castaways. **A human can survive without food for up to two months.** On the contrary, you won't be able to survive without water longer than three to five days. If you don't have any water left, the first thing you should try to avoid is any physical exercise because when you are sweating your body will lose precious fluid. You can stretch your drinking water reserves with a bit of salt water but as soon as you have used up all your fresh water it's getting sketchy. You can drink minimal amounts of salt water – not more than half a liter per day – and thus extend your life time. A test by the French Army showed that the soldiers could survive with nothing but salt water for six days. If you drink more than the half liter you will dry out really fast – the body cannot handle the big amounts of salt, but instead extracts fluid from the cells to dilute the salt water in the stomach.

If you are floating in the ocean with a life vest or without anything at all, you can try to save your energy by laying on the back with straddled legs and arms. If you wear a vest, you can pull the knees up to the chest embracing them with your arms. A technique that is called Heat Escape Lessoning Position or H.E.L.P. – it is the best method to avoid the body from cooling down.

Nobody really knows if a sinking ship can create a swirl that is strong enough to drag people down as the Hollywood movie 'Titanic' suggested. The American TV show 'MythBusters' conducted an experiment and came to the conclusion that such a swirl is nothing but an ancient tale. On the other hand, some survivors have told stories about being dragged under water. **To play it safe you should gain as much distance to a sinking ship as possible.**

SURVIVAL SCHOOL

Imagine your charter boat has sunk somewhere off the coast of Indonesia and you get stranded on a deserted island. Or, you get lost in the jungle while searching for a hidden wave. You are totally on your own and only have the clothes on that are on your back. Don't worry, you will learn how to survive on the following pages.[*]

Finding water

Without any liquid you can only survive for a few days. Coconuts can be your lifesaver as each of them contains about one liter of coconut water. It's pretty easy to open them: First, you need to remove the green, leather-like outer shell which protects the brown coconut with a pointy stone. On one side of the coconut you will find three small, darkish spots – these are the thinnest parts of the shell and it should be no problem to push them in with your pointy stone. If you got a plastic bag with you, you can gain water from any plant: Just put the bag over it and wait. Thanks to the sun, the plant's liquid will evaporate and condensate in the bag, but this trick won't get you more than a few teaspoons of water. The most effective way is collecting rain water with coconut halves. But watch out: Mosquitos love to lay their eggs in there. Before drinking, you should let the water flow through your t-shirt, the fabric works like a natural filter.

Finding food

Reefs are full of mussels and crabs that you can eat without any worries. You should be more careful with eating unknown fruits – there are more poisonous plants on this planet than you might think. If you don't have a choice, you put a piece of the fruit on the inner side of your forearm where the skin is thin and sensitive. Wait for two hours and if your skin doesn't get irritated, you can continue by putting a small piece on your lips. Wait again for two hours, if nothing happens, you put a tiny piece on your tongue for five minutes. Wait again and if you don't feel any change after five to six hours, this probably means you can eat the fruit. However, you can never be 100 percent sure!

Finding fire

Without a lighter, it's going to be tough! You need two pieces of wood that are dry as hay: a flat and softer piece in which you carve a small notch and a solid finger-thick stave of approximately 60 centimeters length. You need to sharpen the stave on one side, put it into the notch and then turn it in between your palms as fast as possible. After a while you will see a bit of smoke coming out of the notch. At this point just add some dry leaves to the ember and you will fuel the fire. You are better off if you have a shoestring or cord with you because you can build a kind of bow with it by tying it to a bench. Interloop it with the stave – if you now see saw the bow, the stave will turn much faster as you would be able to turn it with your palms.

Finding shelter

The skeleton of a little cabin is easy to build, a waterproof roof is much harder to realize. Take a fresh palm leaf (old ones are too dry and will break), fold it up in the middle and weave the long, single leaves together. A roof made of several of these woven palm leaves will keep you dry even during the monsoon rain. A cave offers more protection, but watch out: Never move into a cave close to the ocean as it can turn into a deathly trap during the next big swell or storm.

Finding hope

The feeling of being completely on your own is worse than hunger or thirst. At some point you start thinking that you don't even exist anymore because nobody knows where you are. It might be hard, but try to never give up the hope. Do everything you can to be found: Cut trees and place them on a clearance building the SOS sign. Or build a huge cross made of stones on the highest elevation of the island. There are more airplanes flying around than you can imagine and at some point someone will see your call for help. The day your hope dies will be the day you die, too.

* We sought expert advice from Xavier Rosset who has spent 300 days on a deserted island. On the next page you can read more about his adventures.

How can I survive on a deserted island?

Xavier Rosset knows it. The former Swiss snowboard pro spent 300 days on Tofua, an uninhabited island in the South Pacific.

"After the fisher boat dropped me off on Tofua, a volcanic island in the Pacific, and disappeared into the horizon, my battle for survival started. I had nothing with me except a Swiss Army knife and a machete to help me getting along with the wilderness.

The first thing I did was collect coconuts and try to open them with my machete, but this was harder than it looked. It took 40 minutes until I could finally drink a sip of coconut water! My first big victory that would allow me to at least survive until the next morning. What I didn't know: Too much of the juice acts like a laxative in your body. **In the first two months I almost lost 14 kilograms** – the entire weight I had gained before the start of the expedition to give my body a natural fat reserve.

Besides this, I hadn't taken any specific preparation for my experiment. The first two weeks were really hard: Apart from coconuts, I ate roots, mangos and sometimes mussels. It took three days until I was able to catch my first fish as I had never been fishing before! Luckily, the fishermen that took me to the island had equipped me with a fishing line and some hooks – without this little help, my nutrition would have been a bit one-sided. My self-built cabin only lasted for a few days, more precisely, until the first rain – the roof was not waterproof because I had only loosely laid the palm leaves on each other instead of weaving them together. But the worst thing was the loneliness. After ten days I fell down the black hole, from one second to the next my motivation was gone, like someone had pulled the plug. But I had put myself into this situation and I had to learn to accept it. From this day on I carved a mark into a coconut tree every morning and could then see how the time passed and my goal – 300 days – came closer and closer.

At some point my life on the island became routine and I always had in mind that I had to be very careful in anything I was doing. For emergencies I had a satellite telephone with me, but I knew that it would take days for help to arrive. One day I ran into a wasps' nest in the jungle and carried away five bites. The wasps on the island are way bigger and more poisonous than in Europe, and within an instance I was feeling very bad. I had to vomit and suddenly parts of my body were paralyzed, the poison had the effect of a local anesthetics on my body. After this incident I became much more careful when walking in the jungle. But when it came to natural disasters, I was powerless: During my time on the island I experienced two earthquakes and survived a typhoon. Luckily I had built my camp approximately 60 meters from the beach. Otherwise, I would have been washed away. But nevertheless I made a big mistake: To be able to see the ocean from my cabin, I had cut down all trees in front of it. The storm took charge and unleashed its force on my shelter the whole night – the next morning I was completely soaked and shivering.

The only situation in which I was scared of dying started harmless, with a little cut on my finger. At first, the wound only hurt a bit but soon I couldn't move the hand anymore. I knew I had to do something about it, otherwise the infection would get worse and kill me at some point. Thanks to the satellite telephone I called my doctor in Switzerland and asked him for advice. He explained that the only way to stop the infection was to cut the wound open up to the bone and clean it. A very painful treatment but I didn't have any other choice if I wanted to successfully end my experiment.

I learned a lot during my time on the island. For example, there are things in life you can't change and you should rather use your energy for things you can change; or that often it's the simple moments that are the most magic – the first caught fish, the endless horizon, a night under the stars. Keep your eyes open during your trips and look around – **you will be surprised what you discover."**

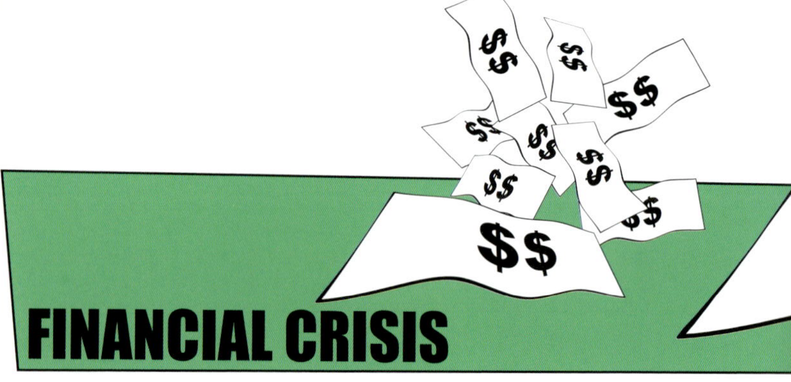

FINANCIAL CRISIS

Broke in the middle of nowhere? No worries, Tom Thumb's* tips will help you get back home:

Hotel rooms – no thanks!

When sleeping outside, moisture and the cold are your worst enemies. Particularly sand can steal a lot of heat which leaves you freezing, even in the tropics. Therefore, a sleeping bag and a plastic groundsheet, like a waterproof poncho or a board bag, are a good idea. Mosquitos can make your night in the nature a nightmare – if I don't have a repellent with me, I smear the juice of wet tobacco all over my skin. Also, snakes can pose a real danger as they like to warm themselves by you as you sleep. So be careful when you awake. Sleeping in towns and cities is more complicated. I don't know why, but it is easier to spend the night on the street in a rich area of the town than in a poor area. It's less likely that you will be chased away – maybe because the police is not used to sleeping backpackers in a rich neighborhood and, therefore, often overlooks them. Apart from that, airports are the ideal place to spend a night. Nowhere else is it more common to see people sleeping in public. In contrast, I don't recommend spending a night in a park. Recreational areas are often the meeting point for small-time criminals and partying teenagers. A cemetery offers great silence in the midst of the city, but the ambiance takes getting used to.

*Tom Thumb's life changed when he turned 20. Back then, he left England for India without a single cent in his pockets. He hitchhiked through France, Germany, Bulgaria, Pakistan and some more countries until he reached Goa to spend a season at the beach. Today he is in his mid-thirties, still traveling, blogging on his website roadjunky.com and writing books about trips without money. If anyone knows how to continue on your trip even though you're broke, it's Tom Thumb.

Restaurant bills – no way!

Getting something to eat for free takes quite an effort. For example, "dumpster diving", which means you search the waste containers behind the supermarkets for food. Getting yourself served on fruit trees could be a more hygienic option. If you are going with the old "coffee trick" you might need to swallow your pride first: Just look out for a self-service restaurant – the bigger and busier, the better –, sip on your pot of coffee for hours and wait until somebody leaves without finishing off their plate – grab it!

Travel costs – no worries!

There is nothing cheaper than hitchhiking, but it's a high art. There are two variations: Either you place yourself next to the street and wait, or you ask people at the gas station. In both cases the driver only has a few seconds to decide if you are a nice guy or an insane serial killer. It definitely helps if you are dressed properly, shaved and smiling. Huge sun glasses, hats and caps are not the best idea if you're trying to establish new contacts. When the driver can't see your eyes, he can't really assess you and might become suspicious of you. A bit of distrust should also be on your side because once you sit in the car, anything could happen to you. Sometimes a driver suddenly demands money for his help, sometimes sex, or he wants to convert you to his religion. To me, hitchhiking is one of the last adventures on this earth.

FIRST-AID KIT

You are standing on the beach looking at your board in disbelief. The big hole in the bottom hadn't been there when you started the first session of your trip only an hour ago. What to do? Do it yourself, give it to a surf shop for repair or just completely ignore the damage? David Kingdon* can't make this decision for you, but he knows exactly which mistakes to avoid. Here is his list:

"Filling the hole with a piece of surf wax is a bad idea. Many think that this procedure will seal a surfboard absolutely waterproof, but that's wrong! A wax-plug will never be 100-percent waterproof and water will still find its way into the core of your board. Even worse is the fact that surf wax is a petroleum product and – like every oil-based product – affects the foam core of a surfboard. First it turns the bright white into an ugly brown, then it wears the material down.

Ignoring the damage? Not good! If you continue surfing your dinged board, water will make its way deeper and deeper into it, spread out and literally start to degrade the foam core. Suddenly, you won't have just one hole at the nose, but another weak spot on one rail or at the tail because the moisture is causing the foam to rot. In the worst case, the water degrades the stringer till your board snaps in two.

Doing it the wrong way, won't pay off: A bit of duct tape will seal a hole for one session, or maybe for the last two days of your trip. Even better is to fill the hole using an instant cure like Solarez, which hardens when exposed to sunlight. But such a repair won't last forever. After maybe five days or so, water will start to leak into the board. If you want to do it properly yourself, then you need a repair kit consisting of two components: resin and hardener. This is the only way the repair will hold as long as the board itself.

Using too much hardener is one of the biggest mistakes you could make. When mixing resin and hardener for a repair, the proportion must be exactly right – otherwise, the mixture could literally burn itself into the foam core while your board starts smoking. That's why you should read the manual and pay attention to the correct proportions. Meanwhile, there are a few two-component repair kits, which are completely foolproof and consist of a powder and a liquid. All you have to do is mix both into the hole of your board. You can't go wrong with it and it lasts really, really long.

Not letting your board dry out is another big mistake. When you start the repair and the foam is still wet inside, there is no chance you will succeed. Even the best shaper won't be able to fix a wet board. Just one night in a warm room is enough to let the foam dry out. Exposing the board to bright sunlight is certainly not a good idea, even if you are in a hurry. The air inside your board could extremely heat up and expand so much that it will cause the fiberglass layer to delaminate from the foam. By the way, the same could happen leaving your board too long inside your parked car during a hot summer day.

Confusing epoxy with polyester resin can easily lead to a total loss. If you try to repair an epoxy board using polyester resin, you will be able to watch the resin eating its way into the foam and increasing a little crack into a huge hole in a matter of seconds. On the other hand, repairing a polyester board using epoxy resin works fine.

*The shaper from England runs his own company "Utopia Surf Factory" in Mimizan on the French Atlantic Coast and has fixed more broken boards over the years than you will probably ever be able to surf in your entire life.

MENTAL ILLUSIONS

You're leaning on the bar of a dodgy joint in downtown Kuta, still stoked from the sunset session. Suddenly, this hot chick appears next to you – she gets so close that not even a piece of paper would fit between your bodies. You feel like a superhero. If only the barkeeper would stop grinning at you so strangely. "Something's wrong", your inner voice warns. But the legs of this beauty are too long, her eyelashes too attractive and her voice too seductive as she whispers in your ear. The Arak drowns your last doubts and the world turns pink until you realize in the hotel room why the barkeeper was constantly smiling at you: The unknown beauty is as masculine as you are. You have been fooled by a lady boy and have to take flight immediately.

Something that could never happen to you? Never say never! The camouflage of a ladyboy, they are called benchong in Bali, is often deceptively perfect. The same goes for a kathoey in Thailand, a muxe in Mexico or a mahu in Hawaii. But there are some signs that could ease your doubts:

If your new acquaintance is **taller than 1.65 meters**, you should look twice. Most Indonesian women are small and petite.

Look out if her **makeup** is overdone. Nothing hides stubble better than a thick layer of powder.

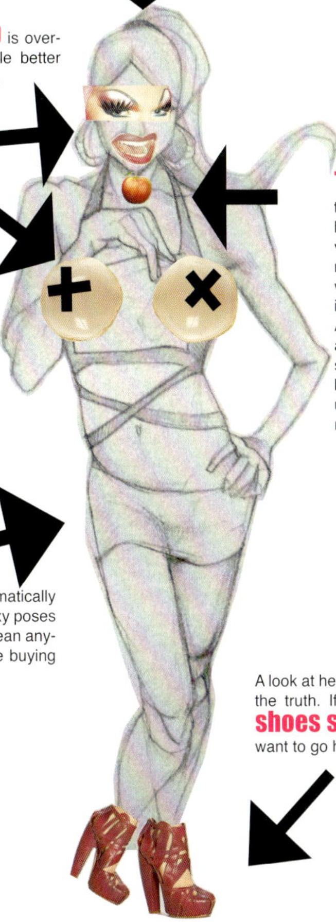

The dark voice is the benchong's achilles heel, it immediately reveals the gender. For this reason, lady boys speak with a soft and whispering voice. A pronounced Adam's apple can be another sign, but it's absence is no guarantee because some lady boys undergo surgery to get it removed.

The "girl" of your dreams has **oversized boobs?** Transvestites love overstatement — when undergoing breast surgery, they tend to choose bigger silicone implants.

Do **her hips** shake dramatically with every step? Are her sexy poses over the top? It might not mean anything, but think twice before buying her another drink.

A look at her feet exposes sometimes the truth. If your lady has a bigger **shoes size** than you, you might want to go home alone.

LOSS CONTROL

Only a few days after his arrival in Bali, Rob Machado was sure: He was cursed. "That morning the sound of the braking waves woke me up before sunrise. The noise was really intense. A huge swell had arrived and as soon as the first sun rays hit the ocean, I was in the water. I was just starting to have fun when I felt that something 'inside' me wasn't alright. I tried to ignore it but it didn't work out. I managed to get on the next toilet just in time, but as soon as I felt a bit of relief, it all started over again. Every 30 minutes I had to run for the toilet, you could have set a watch. At some point I had the idea that it might help going surfing again – wrong decision! It got worse. Now I couldn't leave the toilet anymore. The only thing I could do was to concentrate on my breathing while waiting for the next attack from my guts. The next day the waves were still firing, but my most epic moment was having a bowl of rice – finally I was able to eat again. I didn't even think about surfing – was I cursed and never have a good session in Bali?"

What ruined Rob Machado's surf is known as **"Bali Belly"** to many surfers. In Mexico they call it **"Montezuma's Revenge"**, in India **"Bombay Belly"** and in the Arabian culture it's **"Yalla, Yalla"** which literally means "fast, fast". Most often the cause for the total loss of control over your digestion is a food poisoning. The American Centers for Disease Control estimate that every year about ten million tourists suffer from this, the most common travel-sickness in the world.

There is no bullet-proof protection but there are things you should avoid. For example, drinking tap water in Asia, Africa, South or Central America. If you can, order drinks without ice cubes as you never know if they are made of tap water – you might be safe in popular travel destinations where they mostly use bottled water because it got around that tourists become sick of tap water, but there is no guarantee for that. Salads are a risky meal as well because you can never be sure what water they used to wash the leaves or fruits. Other food is easier to assess. Just watch out that fish, chicken or other meat has been well cooked or fried. If you have any doubts, ask them to put it on the grill once again. A popular advice that always works: Peel it, boil it, cook it – or forget it!

Somehow you were still struck? Try grapefruit seeds – they are said to help fight bacteria, germs, parasites and anything else you can catch on the streets or in the water.

FOUL WATER

Timmy Turner didn't give it a second thought when he went swimming at Huntington Beach that day, he only lived down the road from his home spot and surfed it almost every day. Soon after, he got an ear infection but the pro surfer wasn't too worried. What he didn't know at that time was that the staphylococcus aureus bacteria had already infested his brain. Timmy can't remember the day when his brother Ryan took him to the hospital, but later they told him that everyone thought he was on drugs because he was screaming irrationally and kicking cars. When he arrived in the hospital his brain had already swollen up so much that his right eye was pushed out of the socket. His body temperature hit 41°C and at some point he fell into coma. The bacteria had already eaten through his skull like acid and the only thing the doctors could do was to remove all infected parts leaving Timmy with just one quarter of his skull. His chances of survival were tiny, but almost one year after he had caught the bacteria in the polluted waters off Huntington Beach, Timmy got a new artificial skull. Four weeks later he was surfing again.

Timmy is not the only surfer to get sick after a session at Huntington Beach. It all started in the summer of 1999 when more and more beach go-ers complained about stomach cramps, fever and diarrhea. Water samples assessed that the concentration of bacteria was too high. The surrounding beaches were temporarily closed and experts were hired to find out what had caused this problem. Many accused the sewage plant which was draining off the wastewater of the entire region seven kilometers off the coast of Huntington Beach in a depth of 60 meters. But until today, nobody could prove this theory and the scientists still have no answer as to why, of all places, the beaches of Huntington Beach regularly get haunted by bacteria.

The risks for surfers to catch an infection in polluted water are three times higher than for swimmers. Relatively harmless are diarrhea and stomach pains, but if you are unlucky your next duckdive brings hepatitis A or blood poisoning on you. Besides Huntington Beach, you should also avoid the following beaches:

Padstow, England: The beaches in the southwest of the island belong to the most polluted in Europe. After days of rain the area's canalization becomes flooded and the untreated sewage waters gets washed away into the sea. Normally this should only happen in an emergency case and not more than three times per year. But thanks to global warming, it's raining more than ever before and thus Padstow, as well as many other cities at the coast, have to open their sewage pipes up to 40 times per year.

Port Philip Bay, Australia: Normally lifeguards are busy with saving people from drowning. But at this beach on Australia's south coast they spend their time searching the sand for injection needles, broken glass and other waste. The reason for this are the 300 sewage drains that wash all the Melbourne area's waste into the ocean during flooding. They recently installed filters that catch waste starting from the size of a cigarette stub but they are powerless against the bacteria in the polluted water.

Seminyak Beach, Bali: Due to official regulations, hotels and restaurants need to install their own sewage and canalization system. But most investors shy away from the high costs and so many of the luxury resorts north of Kuta just send their sewage and waste straight into the ocean.

Doheny State Beach, California/ USA: Has to fight similar problems like Huntington Beach and was elected America's most polluted beach three years in a row as the water samples by far exceeded the national critical values. Incidentally, the legendary surf breaks Dana Point and Trestles are just around the corner...

Sandside Bay, Scotland: Dounreay, a nuclear power plant which experienced numerous accidents in the 60s, is located within eyeshot. Still you regularly find radioactive material at Sandside Bay, a popular surf break at the north coast of Scotland. A sign warns tourists about the hazard and only the most hard-boiled surfers paddle out here.

TANDEM RIDE

"This is not gonna work!" you were thinking when you saw the surfer dropping into the wave. The take off seemed way too deep as if he could have escaped the breaking lip. He couldn't. The white water swallowed him and when he surfaced seconds later, his leash was broken and his board gone. But the surfer didn't seem to care; as soon as he realized his situation, he started to swim towards the shore. You have already seen this happen to other people a few times before so no need to take any action, right? Wrong. After a while you notice that the surfer doesn't get any closer to the beach, he is stuck in the rip current. When your eyes suddenly meet you realize his desperation and silent call for help. But do you actually know how to save his life?

Actually, a rescue from the lineup is quite simple. Lifeguards from Australia to Florida use three meter long rescue boards on which they paddle to the drowning victim, drag them up on the board and then get washed to the beach with the white water.

The same technique also works with a shortboard – if you don't have any fears of contact.

Get on board: The person laying on the back of the board needs to put their head on the back of the one in front so that the board lays as horizontal as possible in the water. As the name already suggests, a shortboard is quite short and you need to move together.

Keep going: When the white water or a wave approaches, you both need to paddle as hard as you can.

Hang on: In the white water the board will perform like a wild pony. Maybe the one in the back will get swallowed by the white water for a short moment, but as soon as the board has picked up some speed it will blast out of the white water and you can enjoy the ride to the beach.

PARTY POOPERS

Some things are not mentioned in travel guides. Unfortunately, these secrets often turn out to be pretty unpleasant. Here is a small selection what to expect abroad:

Bears in Canada – are a common sight for Peter Devries, one of the most talented surfers at the Canadian west coast who is constantly on the road, camping along the coast in search for the best waves. "Encounters with bears are normal to me", says Peter. "I grew up here and meeting bears is part of the deal, just as it is with sharks in South Africa." If you tumble over a bear in the forests of British Columbia, you should scream as loud as you can and raise your arms above your head to appear bigger. Running away is a bad idea as it could call up the bear's hunting instinct. Therefore, stay where you are when the animal approaches you. Experts say that most attacks are only bluffs to test the opponent. If you don't have that much luck and the bear decides to go for you, there is only one thing left to do: Get on the ground and curl yourself up like a fetus to protect your vital organs.

Beach shitting in India – is heavy. In 2009, environmental organizations were estimating that half of all the Indian population, about 665 million people, don't have access to sanitary facilities and, therefore, just answer their call of nature outdoors. Thus, each day, 100.000 tons of human excrement end up on fields, streets, beaches or in rivers. Those who have already been to India won't be surprised. On some beaches the ocean smells like a septic tank, the same goes for many rivers, and if you are buying a train ticket for the third class you might witness how the wagon is turned into a public toilet. For some reason, the beaches seem ideal for hundreds of people's morning toilet – if you want to surf here, you should watch for the right tide. The only exceptions are bigger tourist towns as they restrict beach shitting.

Drop-ins in Israel - were something the English pro surfer Sam Lamiroy had to learn the hard way when he visited the Holy Country a few years ago for a movie production. Sam arrived when the swell of the year turned the Mediterranean Sea into surfer's paradise, but he didn't catch one of the set waves - at least not without anyone else on it. "I was waiting for my turn and started to paddle for one of the bigger waves, but when I took off I saw five or six Israeli guys dropping in on me", Sam recalls. "I thought: Well, this can happen. So I waited for another set and once again, everyone was dropping in on me." The same situation happened over and over again, until Sam asked one of the locals about the strange behavior in the lineup. His answer: "It is very rare that we get good waves here so when the moment we all have been waiting for finally arrives, we can't help ourselves but paddle for every wave." In the end, nobody can really ride a wave because there will always be another surfer dropping in.

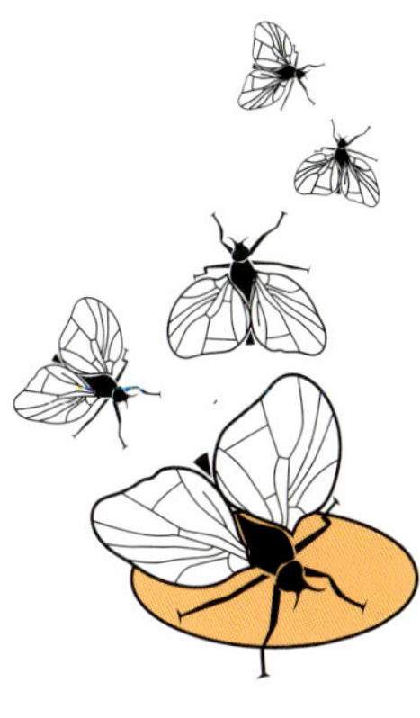

Sandflies in New Zealand – are a spawn out of hell. The tiny beasts, measuring only two to three millimeters, always approach in swarms if not clouds. If you see the first of them, ten others have already bitten you and that's only the beginning of the attack. They ambuscade you anywhere close to water, at the beach, on streams and ponds, on the South Island as well as on the North Island of New Zealand. One of the most prominent victims was Captain James Cook who wrote in his navigation book in May 1773: "The most mischievous animal here is the small black sandfly which are exceeding numerous. Wherever they light they cause a swelling and such intolerable itching that it is not possible to refrain from scratching." The locals have already tried numerous remedies, for example greasing themselves with fish oil or rancid bacon but couldn't really find a bullet-proof protection. On some day tours in areas that are known for sandflies tourists even get advised to put on gloves and headscarfs before exiting the bus.

CRIMINAL MINDS

It always starts pretty unsuspicious, like with this cab ride a few years ago in Venezuela when the surfer asked the driver for a good party place. "Si", he answered: "Good party, I show you!" Without giving it a second thought, the surfer jumped in. The car then left the coast road and started heading towards the inland. The trip didn't seem to end and at some point the surfer started to get worried, but when they arrived in a small village, it became obvious that the driver hadn't lied. All of a sudden they were in the middle of a local festival with bars and music. The surfer dove in and soon noticed that he was the only tourist around. Everyone wanted to start a conversation with him, someone even offered him his daughter for marriage. Then he saw the huge wheel of fortune. As with roulette, you would bet on numbers or colors. But unlike a casino, you would not place chips, but cash. The surfer pulled out a few notes, maybe the equivalent of one or two dollars, and won. He bet a second time and won again. He had caught fire, ordered beer and continued the game. Sometimes he lost, but most of the time he won. After an hour he had collected a serious stack of notes but all of a sudden he started to notice the change: the locals didn't seem to smile anymore, and a strange and uneasy vibe had filled the air. He got worried, in the end he was the only tourist in this little village that he didn't even know the name of and had more money in his pockets than most of the people here probably earned in a month. The surfer only wanted one thing: to get rid of his winnings and he put all the money on one color. Unfortunately, he was unlucky and – won. Instead of a total loss he had carried off even more money. Now he got really frightened. But then a brilliant idea popped up in his mind: He put all cash on the counter of the beer booth and said: "all beers on me". Being disposed of all his earnings, he promptly felt comfortable again.

Not all adventures end so smoothly. Most of the time you only recognize villains after a second glance, for example, if they are confronting you in a police uniform and blaming you for an offense you haven't committed. Or if they are selling you a "brand-new" board and you only notice back home that it had already been snapped.

Villains will try to take you for a ride on every corner – make sure you don't get caught in their trap.

GANGSTER´S PARADISE

There you go: A knife on your throat, a poignant voice next to your ear and your fear of losing more than just your travel budget. How could this happen and what to do now? A glimpse behind the scenes of a robbery:

The offender:

Studies conducted by the Australian police state that there are four different types of offenders that commit robberies. You are a lucky chap if you are confronted by a offender of the "ordinary people" group: Fathers or housewives, people that normally would not commit a crime, but who are so desperate that they don't see any other possibility. These offenders want to pull off the robbery as fast and inconspicuously as possible, therefore, they avoid violence. The second group are drug addicts that try to feed their addiction. They are probably the most dangerous offenders because they are often unpredictable and act irrational. Furthermore, they are so desperate that they are willing to do anything. The so-called "thrill seekers" commit crimes out of boredom: teenagers or young adults that gather in groups and rob liquor stores or tourists to get their hands on money for alcohol. The chances to meet an offender of the fourth group is pretty rare: professional gangsters who live off their crimes. They know exactly what they want and how to get it.

The victim:

Bandits don't choose their victims by accident. Those who look rich and seem easy to overpower, are ideal. For example, a surfer who stumbles out of a bar totally drunk, or even better, searches for the next cash machine. How a robbery takes place always depends on the situation. In a dark and secluded alley, they might point a weapon at you and demand your money; or they knock you out first and only then ask for valuables. In the public, the robbery happens as fast as a flash – within the blink of an eye, they snatch your cell phone, camera or wallet from you and escape. Sometimes they try to get you involved in a conversation while getting as close to your valuables as possible. The FBI says that approximately half of all robbery victims experience physical violence. Of these, 20 percent are in need of medical help after the robbery and six percent of all homicides are registered as robbery homicide.

The strategy:

"Never offer any resistance" – this is at least what the state departments advise in case of a robbery in Honduras, El Salvador or Mexico. In these countries, weapons are as common as the willingness to use them. An advice that is shared by the South-African scientist Rudolph Zinn who has interviewed several offenders for his book 'Home Invasion' and found out more about their perception. A reluctant victim that is not handing out the money, makes the offender become suspicious, thinking that the victim might deprive him of a few dollars or valuables. So, the next step would be to break this reluctance with physical violence. It is better to stay calm, not address the offender, show your open hands and follow any instructions. It might be even seen as provocative if you maintain eye contact. Never ever vent your anger with insults, the youngest robber and murderer that Zinn interviewed for his book was 13 when he shot his victim; as a reason he stated that the victim, "hasn't respected me as a man."

HUNTING SEASON

Tourists are an easy prey and the creativity in ripping them off seems unlimited – this is at least what a story by Tom Thumb, one the world's most experienced backpackers and founder of roadjunky.com, suggests. He wrote about two German girls who got approached by a local soon after their arrival in Delhi, India. The man was very friendly and described his family's guesthouse in the greatest details: a house boat on the lake of Dal in the province Kashmir, including a stunning view on the Himalaya. He was so convincing that the girls took on the 36 hour trip to the lake. Everything was perfect – until the boat took off. All of a sudden the family seemed seriously concerned and told the girls about new armed conflicts in the province: there were shootings and dead bodies on the streets. It would be too dangerous for the girls to go on land, they certainly would be kidnapped or shot. But as long as they would stay on board, they were fine and not in danger. However, the prices for food had quadrupled due to the conflict. This went on for three weeks, then the girls were broke. As luck would have it, the conflict just ended exactly at the same time and it had become safe for them to leave the boat.

It requires lots of imagination to think up such a civil war scenario. Three of the most popular tourist traps are based on more simple plans:

Cars with a life of their own

How it works: One morning your rental car stops after a few hundred meters and doesn't start again. Coincidentally, a few locals pass by and introduce themselves as car mechanics. Within minutes they detect the problem, solve it and demand an exorbitant amount of money for their help.

What do do: It is obvious that the friendly mechanics sabotaged the car the night before. They didn't really damage anything, but only branched off a cable or a line. If you know a bit about cars, you should be able to detect the problem yourself. In Indonesia almost any older rental car has a filter in its fuel withdrawal line – if your car stops after a few hundred meters, you should check out if they branched off the line right at this spot.

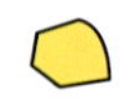

Money changer with false bottom

How it works: The result is always the same: You don't get enough money for your dollars. The procedure can vary: Some money changers use manipulated calculators that miscalculate to your disadvantage. Others drop some notes while counting them, and sometimes you get bills that have become invalid since the last currency reform.

What do do: If the money changer is offering a better exchange rate than the banks, something must be wrong. They couldn't realize profit without ripping you off – avoid them!

The deal of your life

How it works: In Sri Lanka or India it's gems, in Arabic countries it's gold or jewelry – merchandise you don't know much about. But this doesn't matter because as soon as the seller has taken you in, you smell the deal of your life. It seems to be so simple: Just buy some gold or gems for a cheap price here and sell them at home for much more. The merchant explains to you everything by showing the international price lists – you just need to take your chance. But if you do, you will get caught in the trap.

What do do: Be honest to yourself and resist the temptation of making a fast buck! You have no clue if the merchant's gems are really precious or not, and you also don't know if his prices are okay or pure fantasy.

BUYER´S GUIDE

It happens all the time: evil surf shop owners betraying their clueless customers by telling them that a second hand board is almost new and has been only surfed once, while in reality the last session snapped it into two pieces. These bandits know all about hiding dings or damages, but you can unmask their words as lies quite easily by following the advice of shaper David Kingdon*:

"No visible repairs doesn't mean there hasn't been any reparation at all. Every shaper knows many visual tricks. That goes as far as covering the whole top of a surfboard with a thin layer of tinted resin – resin with added color pigments. The resin hides really everything from a deep hole to a clean snap in the middle. But this technique means a lot of effort, so only a few use it. Most give the board just a little spray job and hide the damage under a colored ribbon, which runs around the board, or maybe a big star somewhere on the board. In any case, if a spray job hides only a little bit of the stringer, be suspicious!

It's not only the look that could be revealing, it's also the weight. Every surfer has a feeling for what's normal and what's too heavy for a surfboard. Just grab the board you are about to buy and consider whether the weight feels normal to you. If a board was snapped in two pieces, you need a lot of resin to fix it and that makes a board way heavier. The difference is so evident that you should instantly detect it.

Another trick even better reveals a hidden damage. Just lift the board exactly in the middle on one rail and see what's happening. If the nose or tail sink a little bit to one side, there must be something wrong – probably the board saw a bigger repair which makes one end heavier than the other. Normally, the board must be completely balanced out and stay dead horizontal.

It also helps to look closely along the rails from the nose to the tail or vice versa. A board that was already snapped will have some visible dents or maybe a slight bump along its outline, because even the best shaper won't redo a broken board as perfect as it was. Any surfboard, that was seriously damaged will keep some marks – you just have to find them."

*The shaper from England moved to Mimizan on the French Atlantic coast some years ago where he runs his own company "Utopia Surf Factory". In a blink of an eye he can tell you whether your new "second hand" board was a rip-off or a good deal.

THEFT PREVENTION

Crime scene 'surf camp': It happened on a windy night in October. The rain was slashing against the windows of the surf camp in Portugal, and at 11 p.m. all surfers had retreated to their rooms around the patio. The house was built like a wild west fort with only one main door leading in. That's why everyone felt pretty safe in this little bubble isolated from the rest of the world. However, it was only an illusion, as the thieves that entered the building that same night proved. The clacking window shutters and the howling wind offered the intruders a perfect setting while they snatched up the wetsuits hanging outside on the patio and disappeared undetected into the pitch-black night with their swag.

Crime scene 'beach': The session at Bali's Legian Beach had been long. Since the surfer had ridden his first wave in the morning, hours had passed. Now the merciless midday sun was baking down and the surfer retreated into the shade of a palm tree. He was not alone, but surrounded by beach sellers, tourists and locals. While observing the buzz of activity and feeling the soft offshore wind stroking his face, he nodded off. He had placed his board right next to him, but when he woke up 30 minutes later, it was gone. Someone had stolen the board, even though it had been only an arm's length away, while he was laying on a busy stretch of beach crowded with people.

Crime scene 'camping site': One week has passed since he had removed the back seats of his car and started heading towards France. He had parked his car under the pine trees in a camping site right behind the sand dunes. During the night, he slept inside the car – unfortunately, the car was too small to fit both him and his board. But he didn't just put the board on the roof of his car. Instead, he laid it underneath, left the trunk open and fixed the leash inside the car next to his head. Any thief would have had to get inside the car to open the leash – nobody would dare to come that close, he reassured himself. But one morning he woke up with the leash cut and the board gone.

Three stories that demonstrate that you should never feel too safe. No matter where you are and how unlikely it might seem – someone has probably already checked you and your belongings out. During the main season, tourist areas are the most dangerous as they draw beach goers like moths to the flame. Surfers are well received victims because boards and wetsuits can fetch high prices. The only thing you can do is to watch like a hawk and never let down your guard. Thieves wait for exactly this loophole and tuck in.

SPECIAL EXPENSES

A warning to begin with: All the later mentioned transactions officially never happened. However, they somehow exist, and according to the tales of many traveling surfers they always follow the same pattern, no matter if you are in Indonesia, Nicaragua, Sri Lanka or Mexico.

The problems always start when you get behind the steering wheel of your rental car or on your motorbike. The best solution to avoid an encounter with the police's twilight economy would probably be to abstain from any wheels. But having said that, many spots would be out of reach for you.

Next, your opponent, a police officer that is well-positioned at the side of the road, enters the stage. You have no idea why he is waving at you and forcing you to stop. At this moment, the cop, too, still might have no idea, but he will quickly find a reason. Maybe you haven't buckled your seatbelt, maybe it's your surfboards on the roof, maybe he just wants to check your international driver's license or maybe he just says you were driving too fast.

The next act of the game reads: intimidation. The cop says that your offense is serious and in case he has stopped you in front of the police station, he will ask you to follow him inside. Separated from your friends and confronted by a police officer in a foreign country, even the most experienced globetrotter will start to feel queasy. However, the entire procedure is pure calculation! But how can you exit this game, or better, how can you avoid getting involved in it at all?

There are a few roles you can play:

The blind driver: Of course, a waving police officer at the side of the road is not easy to overlook, but just ignore him, look straight and don't slow down. These tactics pretty much always work and in case the police goes after you, you can still stop and claim that you didn't see anyone.

The understanding tourist: You have stopped and are now facing the cop. Over and over again he claims the seriousness of your offense and explains to you how long it takes to see a judge – certainly a few days, maybe even weeks. Now it's time for your part! Be understanding, regret your offense and ask him the magic question: "Is there any possibility to sort out this situation here and now?" You can bet there will be one...

The broke surfer: A role that helps to reduce the fine for your offense to a minimum. But you need to take a few preparations before: Place a few bills in your pocket and hide the rest of your money somewhere else. When the cop offers you to pay the fine, which certainly will be more than you are expecting, directly to him, just get the bills out of your pocket and claim: "This is all I have."

Rookie mistakes you should avoid:

Panic! Just tell yourself that you haven't really committed any offense, even though the cop might insist that you did. Stay cool and see the entire situation as a kind of business transaction.

Disrespect! Police officers expect the rest of the world to respect their authority. Why risk needless trouble that might even result in a higher fine when telling the cop what you think of him? Never use the word "bribe", but instead use "fine".

Ignorance! Don't think these tricks will work in Europe, the USA or Australia! If you ignore the stop sign of a police officer in one of these countries, you probably end up in the evening news.

HAPPY TRAVEL

Like waves, surfers travel. Either because they live inland or because they enjoy leaving the comfort zone of their local break to explore new shores. In both cases you end up sitting in the car for days, spending hours on obsolete trains or flying around the world. And for what? To be able to surf for 24 minutes! That's the total amount of time an average surfer spends on a wave during a surf trip. Consider a 16 day trip, which is quite common for someone employed: Take two days for arrival and departure and you have 14 days left. If you consider flat or rest days, you might end up with 12 days. With an average of two sessions per day, you get 24 sessions per trip. Most of us will spend two hours in the water in which, depending on the conditions, we will maybe ride 10 waves. One ride rarely lasts longer than six seconds, which means one minute of surfing in total per session. So you spend 24 minutes per trip actually riding your surfboard. That doesn't sound like much fun. However, for these 24 minutes, we book 16 hour flights, stay in dodgy hostels and squeeze ourselves into cramped busses that would have been retired in Europe 20 years ago. So why are we doing this to ourselves? Because 24 minutes of stoke are worth more than a two weeks stay in a 5 star hotel in Egypt.

To get the best out of these 24 minutes, you should consider some preparation. Nothing is more annoying than getting your board out of the bag, only to notice that the baggage handlers have taken their toll, or going over the falls on any wave because your body is not ready.

It's all about being prepared – in life as well as on the road.

LUGGAGE INSPECTION

Essentials that can save your trip:

Earplugs: Provide help in many situations! For example, when the baby in the row in front of you screams from the departure in Paris until the arrival in Agadir, at 5:25 am when the night train (only ten meters away) passes by your bungalow in Sri Lanka resembling a nightly earthquake or when the Aussie guy in the room next to you in Kuta starts snoring at the same volume of a saw mill after his tenth bintang.

Replacements: Fins break, leashes tear and fin keys just vanish. Most of the time this happens at the worst moment – when the waves are pumping. Make sure you have replacements with you. Nothing sucks more than driving around for days looking for a new fin at the end of the world while your friends are surfing one epic session after the next.

Duct Tape: Without this super strong tape, the astronauts wouldn't have been able to repair the damaged Apollo 13 capsule in 1970 and return safely to earth. During the Vietnam War US pilots patched up the rotor blades of their helicopters with this tacky magic bullet. Proof enough that duct tape keeps up with your expectations. No matter if you have to fix your torn board bag, seal a hole in your rail or fix the bandage on the laceration of your foot.

Superglue: The product of choice for many pro surfers in case they cut their foot open with a fin, bite through their lip with one of their teeth or get injured some other way. In fact, superglue is already officially admitted for surgical dressing in the US for years and especially recommendable for long and narrow cuts. But don't forget to disinfect the wound first!

Betadine: Is only one of many substances available as ointment, powder or liquid that is used for the disinfection of small wounds. It doesn't matter which one you choose, as long as you carry one with you because an inflamed wound is the last thing you wish for.

Wedding ring: Only interesting for female surfers. Nothing keeps persistent admirers at arm's length on the beaches of Bali, Sri Lanka or somewhere else in Asia more than a fake wedding ring.

WRAPPING ART

A funny story is circulating about the Australian surf legend Mark Occhilupo: One day he arrived at the airport carrying a brand-new stick, that hadn't even seen a wax job, and just handed the blank board – with no bag or any other protection – to the staff at the check-in counter. We don't know what the board looked like when in arrived in Hawaii, but being a professional surfer, Occy could have coped even with a total loss. You, on the other hand, shouldn't shy away from investing in a board bag.

1 Size: If your bag is too tight, maybe so tight that the fabric is full of tensions after you closed the zipper, then the bag loses all its cushion and every impact will directly hit your board. Furthermore, you risk the zipper to blow off somewhere on the airport and your belongings to be scattered all over the runway. On the other hand, if your bag is too big, your boards will fly around inside and have to absorb more impacts than necessary. The perfect bag leaves a two finger wide space all around the board.

2 Rails: Most damages are found on the nose or tail, the rails come in second place. Dane Gudauskas protects them with a few towels squeezed inside his bag. Bubble warp is functional and quite common as well. If you are a perfectionist, look for pipe insulation, cut these soft foam-tubes in the middle and pad them around your rails.

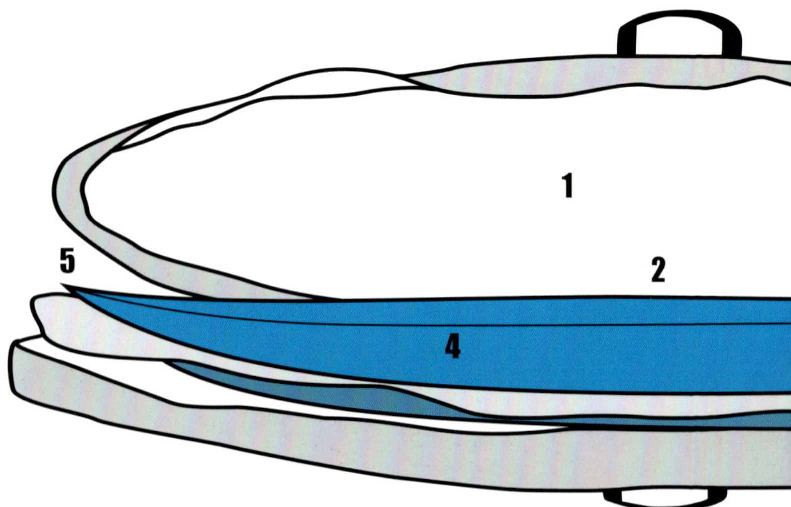

3 Fins: Before heading to the airport, you should certainly remove the fins. But don't throw them carelessly in your board bag. Fins are made of much more solid material than the board and their sharp edges can cause some awkward dings if flying around inside the bag. In case you are still surfing glassed-on fins, you should definitely invest time into protecting them; a block of styrofoam that covers all three fins might be the best way to do it.

4 Check-in: Never forget, you only got ONE, only ONE board with you – regardless of how many boards you really packed and how big your bag looks. You will get away with this white lie at most airports and in fact only be charged for one board. Maybe you will be caught with your pants down one day (in Bali every board bag that looks a bit suspicious will be opened to count the boards inside), but even then you won't have to pay more than what you would have been charged anyway.

5 Nose & Tail: When the Californian pro Dane Gudauskas is leaving for a surf trip, he usually packs three or four boards. At the bottom of the bag Dane always starts with his longest board building the other ones in a pyramidesque shape upon it, finishing with the shortest board on top. To give a little extra protection to the noses and tails, Dane stuffs pillows (that he sometimes grabs from hotel rooms) in the front and the back of his bag. Some surfers swear by bubble wrap, others use styrofoam blocks and hollow them out to fit the shape of their boards' noses or tails.

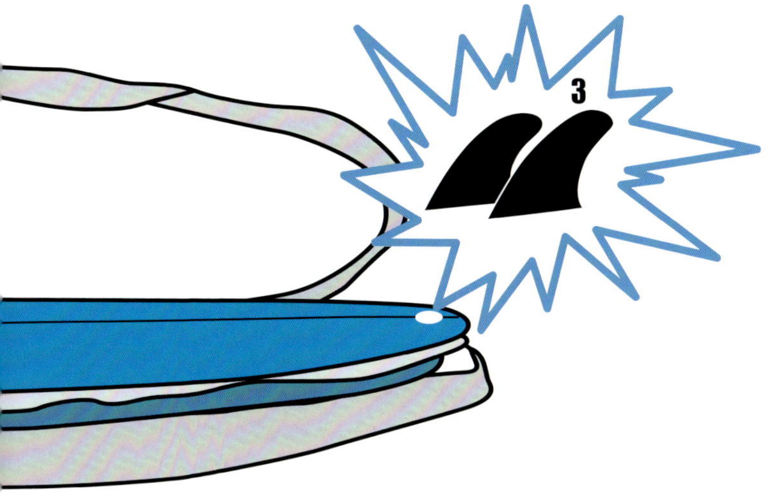

FLIGHT SCHOOL

The longest flight in the world takes 18 hours and 30 minutes: nonstop from New York to Singapore. Flying from Europe to Australia or the other way around includes a few stop-overs and often means that you are sitting in a plane for 20 hours or more. A torture for your body – but not if you follow some simple rules.

The dressing rule: Tracksuit bottoms are much more comfortable than jeans, but if you look handsome, you will have better chances for an upgrade at the check-in in case the flight is overbooked. If you are not that lucky and end up in the economy class, you should line up at the end of the queue when the boarding starts. If you enter the plane last you see which seats are not booked, and with a bit of luck you will get an entire middle row for yourself, which is almost as comfortable as a bed.

The water rule: Thanks to modern air conditioning, the air inside a plane is as clean as in an operating room. Nevertheless, a study conducted by the Journal of Environmental Health Research says that it is 100 times more likely to catch a cold on board of a plane than in daily life. The reason: The air humidity inside a plane's cabin is only rated at 10 percent during a flight (50% would be normal). Unfortunately, the dry air harms our nose and throat mucous membranes that normally act as a natural barrier protecting us from germs and viruses. The solution: Drink as much water as possible! Frequent fliers also swear by salt water nasal spray.

The fiber rule: The higher the plane ascends, the lower the air pressure inside the cabin. If you take an inflated balloon with you on board, it will approximately expand 30 centimeters on a flying altitude of 10.000 meters. The same happens to the air inside your bowel resulting in flatulence. Fibers boost this body function and are frequently included in the board menu (noodles and bread). Rather eat vegetables and only a bit of meat or fish – you will feel a lot better and less sluggish which will have positive results on your first session.

The jet lag rule: Probably no one knows better about how to quickly adjust your body to different time zones than flight attendants. They live by a simple rule: If they arrive at the final destination before 1 p.m., they go to sleep for not more than three hours, then get up again and go to bed at their normal time at night. If they arrive after 1 p.m. they try to stay awake as long as possible – but never go to bed before 7 p.m.!

SEATING CHART

No matter where you are sitting in an airplane, you always have the feeling that the others have a better seat. You can change this by doing your reservation online and choosing yourself. The quality of a seat depends on the airplane type and the airline, but some tips are valid everywhere.

- The seats at the emergency exit offer the most seat pitch but often cost extra; but you can still try and ask at the check-in if these seats are still available. You should avoid the row in front of the emergency seats as you won't be able to turn your seat back down.

- If you suffer from fear of flying, you should better place yourself on the seats above the wings – here, turbulence and vibrations are the fewest.

- The seats in front of the toilets are the worst on the entire airplane: You will have to deal with displeasing smells, high sound level and seats backs that can't be adjusted.

- Statistics about plane crashes prove: Those sitting in the back have greater chances of survival.

- The seats in front of the engines are more noisy than the ones behind.

PS: The most seat pitch on long-haul economy class flights are offered by Thai Airways (91 cm), then Emirates or Air China (both 86 cm). American Airlines (76 cm) offers the least space.

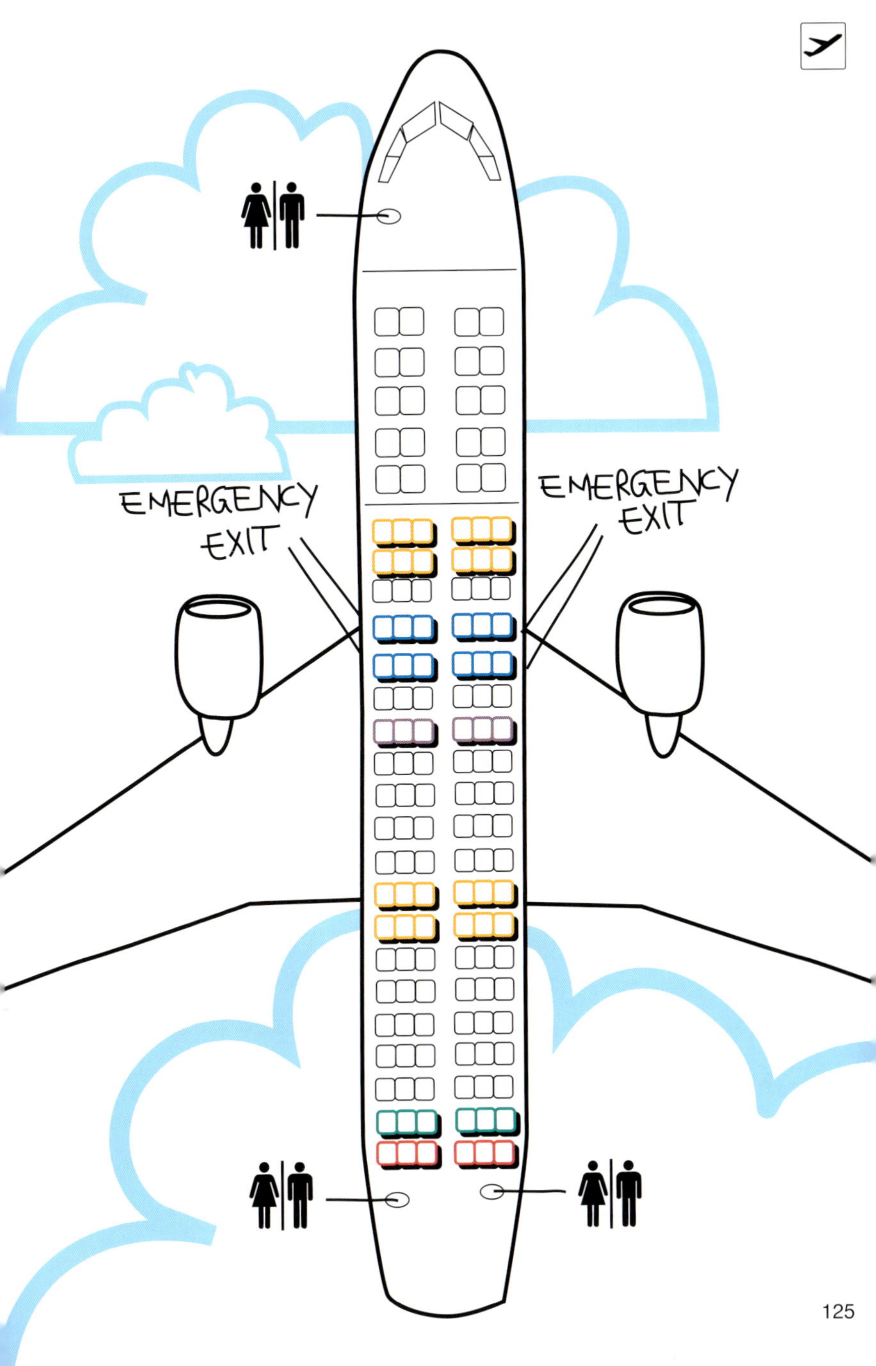
EMERGENCY EXIT
EMERGENCY EXIT
125

MUSCLE WORK

Every surfer that only gets in the water one or two times per year, knows the feeling: The first session after four months and your entire body hurts – the shoulders, the back, the neck. You feel like a granny, and the next day you can barely move because your muscles are totally sore. This goes on for days and when you just start to feel fit again you have to head back home. If you are tired of this, you should either move to the ocean or prepare your body. We* have put together the four ultimate yoga exercises for surfers that you can do at home, on the beach or even in the lineup.

Locust Pose

How to get there: Lay down on your board bag and activate the buttocks muscles while also engaging the quadriceps (thighs) and the lower back. Start by raising the chest off the ground and follow with the legs. Activate the arms by drawing the shoulder blades together and back towards your hips. Hold for between three and seven breaths and repeat twice.

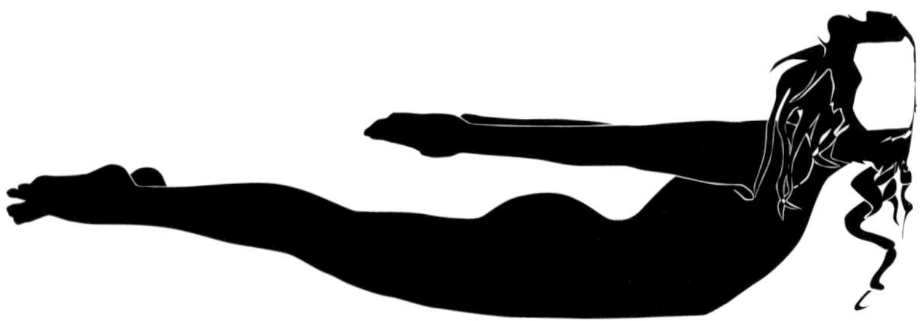

The benefits: Strengthens the muscles that arch the back preparing your body for paddling, the activity that lets most surfers down when away from waves for long periods of time.

*Roland Wimbush shared his expert knowledge with us. The Australian started surfing when he was 10 years old and currently lives on the French Atlantic coast. Here, the 38 year old has founded his own clothing company and is teaching yoga for surfers (www.chocloproject.com). A few pages further he reveals what you can do in advance to prepare your body for surf trips.

Eagle Pose

How to get there: Open arms out to the side, shoulder height. Cross the right arm over the left arm, then bend at the elbows and wrap the hands around bringing the palms together. The trick here is to guide the hands up while dropping the shoulder down and away from the ears giving you a deep stretch between the shoulder blades. On an inhale take the hands towards the sky and on the exhale drop the shoulders away from the ears. Once you have held for six breaths release and take to the other side. Doing the full version, you additionally cross the left leg over the right and wrap the heel around the opposing calf. From here, slowly bend your knees more and drop your hips, increasing the intensity of the stretch. Be careful never to lower your hips lower than your knees. This pose is tricky to start with, but progress and benefits come very quickly. Hold each side for between five to ten breaths each time going deeper and holding longer.

The benefits: The seated variation can be practiced everywhere: in the plane, airport or in the water waiting for a set. It gives you a great shoulder and upper back stretch releasing any tension you may have after a long session. It is also a great preparatory stretch to increase flexibility and stabilize the shoulders. The full Eagle position will work on your balance, leg strength and stability while providing a deep stretch in the buttocks muscles and psoas, a very important muscle that links our vertebrae to the hips. This muscle is particularly hard to reach, but very important for surfers as it is what gives us our mobility in the hips, the key to radical maneuvers and a fluid style.

Open Chair Pose

How to get there: From a standing position, bend your legs as though you were about to sit on a chair while bringing your palms together in front of your chest on an inhale. Be careful not to drop your hips lower than your knees in order to protect the latter. On an exhale twist hook your left elbow over your right knee keeping your hands in front of your chest and on an inhale open your arms to expand the chest and shoulders using the contact of your left elbow against your right knee to go deeper in your stretch. On an exhale release the stretch and lower your chest to your knees and allow your hands to drop down towards the ground either with straight or bent legs depending on your flexibility. On an inhale raise hands above the head with your knees still bent and repeat on the other side. For best results, repeat two to three times on each side.

The benefits: Stretches the spine from the bottom to the top, improves digestion and increases elasticity, flexibility, circulation and nutrition to spinal nerves, vessels and tissues. Increases synovial fluid of the joints and helps prevent slipped discs. Not only will it help with lower back pain caused by paddling but it will also increase the amplitude you get out of your turns thanks to improved elasticity in the spine. This exercise is also a great way to build strength and balance in the legs while getting a great stretch in the hamstrings and lower back.

Tricep and Shoulder Stretch

How to get there: In a seated or cross-legged position take hold of your leash. Holding on to the end of it raise your right arm over your head and then bend at the elbow allowing your hand to drop behind your head. Bend your left hand behind your back and take hold of the leash where ever is comfortable for you, slowly and gently working your way up each time you practice. Repeat on the other side holding for between five and ten breaths each time.

The benefits: This stretch is fantastic for releasing tension in the triceps and fronts of shoulders; the muscles used in the take off.

TRAINING SCHEDULE

"For three years, I was living in Annecy, in the heart of the French Alps. During that time, my few surf trips always followed the same pattern: In the first three days every part of my body was aching, I was really tired and desperately calling for a day off surfing", the Australian surfer Roland Wimbush recalls. Today he has moved back to the ocean, but he still knows what it feels like only being able to go surfing one or two times per year. At some point he had enough of this torture and decided to change something: He started to shape his body during the time in between the trips. Here he tells what his workout looked like – imitation strongly recommended!

Swimming:

Great for your cardio, and it requires the same muscles as paddling does – muscles that we don't really use in daily life. You work all the muscles you need to, in your shoulders, in your back, in your neck. And it is something you can build on: If you start swimming one to two months before you go on the trip, maybe two to three times a week, you will quickly see results. Start with ten laps and slowly build it up to 50, and at some point 100 laps won't be a problem anymore. In the beginning you won't be used to the swimming and the breathing but then you get to the coast and it makes a huge difference: You will still feel tired for a few days because you are not used to the constant exposure. However, it won´t get to the point where you feel you need a break after two or three days and you have to stop for a day. Thanks to swimming, your body is used to the work, your muscles won't ache anymore and you will be able to easily enjoy a second session per day.

Strength training:

I complement the swimming with a bit of strength training. But don't think lifting weights: If you are only doing weights, like bench pressing, it is only building up the big muscles, but not the little muscles that support your joints – overstressing of your joints, back and shoulder problems will be the result. Often people who do not surf on a regular basis get small injuries after a few days of surfing because their body is not used to the continuous action of paddling. If you train the little stabilizing muscles, you won´t hurt yourself anymore. The best thing to do this is a swiss ball. Surfers like Mick Fanning and Taylor Knox swear by this specific training that trains stability, flexibility and balance at the same time. If you are doing push ups on these balls, you are using much more muscles in your body than you would doing push ups on the ground. You can intensify the push ups and improve your balance at the same time if you do a push up on the ball and alternate lifting your legs with each push up. Surfing involves a lot of twisting, so balance poses on the side are very useful: Do a side-push and put the ball in between your legs, this strengthens the core muscles you need for powerful turns.

Yoga:

Even though I'm already 38 I have never been surfing any better: I can surf longer and with more endurance than years ago. Why? I think the main reason is yoga: A lot of yoga poses are similar to motions you do when surfing, but most important is that yoga is all about working on your alignment and bringing everything symmetric again, working both sides equally. Most things we do are asymmetric; if you are right footed or right handed your body eventually creates imbalances. At 20 you haven't had much time to create many imbalances, there might be an imbalance in your hips but it won't be really affecting you until later on. By the time you get to 30 or 40 your body is so used to that position that it is very hard to break it down and start again. The problems usually start in your hips and then spread to your shoulders, your legs or knees. Furthermore, surfing is a very asymmetric sport: You are either a regular or goofy surfer and, therefore, one side of the body is always getting pushed harder. Yoga makes everything symmetric again and, therefore, prevents your posture from getting imbalanced due to one-sided exposure. A problem often caused by surfing! Paddling builds up your lower back, but it doesn't really train your stomach. That's why a lot of Australian surfers over 50 have a really exaggerated bend in the lower back (often exaggerated with the help of a beer belly) – this obviously has an effect on your surfing and results in back problems at some point. If you regularly do yoga you will able able to surf at 50 the same way you did at 30 (just look at Taylor Knox). This is as important for surfers living at the ocean as it is for someone who only gets in the water one or two times per year."

GOURMET KITCHEN

Professional surfers live off their sports. Their body is an investment they want to tune like a subtle instrument. They know that carrots and fish are healthier than chips and hamburgers, but there is more you can do to improve your diet.

Powerful root

The Brazilian **Carlos Burle** became the first Big Wave World Champion in 2010, and is fitter in his 40s than many 20 year olds. His secret? Two-fisted training six days a week and a small root growing in the Peruvian Andes: Maca. The Incas already knew about the plant's performance-enhancing effects. It is said that the Maca root contains precious nutrients that stimulate the immune system and improve the endurance. Carlos Burle swears by the exotic vegetable that is dried, ground and then sold as powder: "Every day I'm having a bowl of oatmeal mixed with fruits, nuts and one table spoon of Maca for breakfast. A great nutrition basis for strenuous hours of surfing and training."

Raw food

When facing **Brain Conley**, you hardly believe that this haggard guy is capable of surfing waves that can break your neck. But he is – thanks to his "raw power" diet, a specific nutrition that grants the surf pro super hero energy. The 31 year-old American hasn't eaten anything boiled or fried for years now, steaks are nothing but "dead carcasses" to him. Instead Brian only eats fresh fruits, nuts as well as vegetables and drinks his "green superfood", a fresh squeezed orange juice mixed with algae and diverse other plants. To him there are no exceptions, not even when he is flying to the other end of the world to surf a wave. " The hardest place to be is at home in California as whole foods are really expensive there. When I´m traveling I eat for free most of the time. Like if we're in the tropics I'm in paradise, because I can go climb a coconut tree or find papaya or mangos." His emergency ration: A bag full of nuts, they contain a lot of fat and provide huge amounts of energy. What is really stunning is that Brian's raw food diet even protects him from the sun: "I never apply any sunscreen. The sun is a natural detoxifier. You only get sunburned when your body contains toxics that the sun brings up."

Milk diet

In 1992, at the age of 20, he became the youngest world champion of all time and in 2011, at 39, the oldest. Not the only record **Kelly Slater** is holding: No one else before him won eleven world championships titles. How does he do it? What sets him apart from his competitors that are often ten, fifteen years younger? Maybe his dislike of dairy foods? They weaken our bodies and make us sick, he states in his book "For the Love" where he explains his theory: "In the 1930s a doctor named Francis Pottenger started a ten-year study on 900 cats. One group was fed with raw whole milk, while the other group had nothing but pasteurized whole milk. The raw milk group thrived, but the pasteurized milk group became listless, confused, and highly vulnerable to a number of degenerative ailments we'd normally associate with humans, like heart disease, kidney failure, thyroid dysfunction, and brittle bones. The offspring of the pasteurized group were all born with poor teeth and weak bones, a sure sign of calcium deficiency, which indicated a lack of calcium absorption from the milk. The third-generation produced even worse results than the pasteurized group, with many stillborn and the rest born sterile, so ended the experiment. At the time this research was conducted, pasteurized milk was a recent introduction. Up to this point humans had thrived on raw milk. Today, it is illegal to sell raw milk in many parts of the world. We now have a third-generation of humans taking part in the big pasteurized milk experiment, and just like Dr. Pottenger's cats, we are not looking good. Infertility and calcium deficiency are major and growing problems."

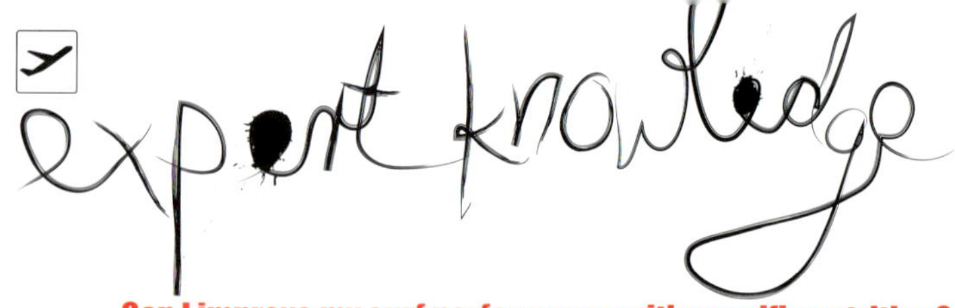

Can I improve my surf performance with specific nutrition?

Of course, says Doctor Jan Willms – he is a surfer himself and has launched dietary supplements specifically made for water and mountain sports.

"Going on surf trips means a lot of stress on your body as you are demanding maximum performance for weeks. You have to deal with long-haul flights and different time zones, have to adapt to tropical climate or cold water and want to enjoy at least one session per day. To prepare your body for this exceptional situation, a healthy diet with vegetables, fruits and whole foods is often not enough. Furthermore, the food supply in various isolated surf areas is not very diversified. For example, in Central America, rice and beans dominate the menu which is tasty, but doesn't provide your body with all the necessary nutrients to go full speed ahead. So what do you do when a perfect, hollow left is breaking right in front of you but you are too weak to even pull on your rash guard?

This is what happened to me in 2009: I was traveling to Australia, Indonesia and across Europe – never had I been surfing more in my life. In fact, I should have been fit as a fiddle but instead I felt tired and suffered from many colds. I started to read into dietary supplements but there was no product on the market that could come up to my requirements. Therefore, I composed the substances I was looking for myself and it worked: I had more paddle power and was recovering faster after each session. The idea of NiceOne was born: Dietary supplements that are specifically made for surfers and other extreme sports athletes.

It's easy to explain: If you are having a snack after a session it takes the body three to six hours to digest the nutrients and transport them to their site of action, for example the muscles. During this period of time, it is very likely that you had been in the water for a second time, this time wondering why your arms feel as heavy as lead despite your little power snack. That's where NiceOne Recovery jumps in: Little tabs that contain amino acid, minerals and vitamins, targeted to improve the strength endurance that is quite important in surfing. At cyber-speed – within one hour – the substances supply the body with everything you need to get your shutdown systems working again. But our planet provides more magic bullets: reishi for example, a special kind of mushroom that is already used in Japan and China for more than 4000 years and strengthens the body's defenses.

This is essential at the beginning of a surf trip as the performance of the immune system declines in the first days due to the unknown exposure and the long journey. Scientific studies have proven that the mushroom improves the white blood cell's activity thus strengthening the body's defenses. Besides your body, you also need your brain for surfing. **What helps is some rhodiola, a traditional medical plant that grows 2000 meters above the sea level in the Alps**. The plant acts like a natural energy drink which stimulates your nervous system over a long period of time – perfect when the waves are pumping and you are staying in the water for hours.

We are especially proud on our 'sunscreen to swallow'. Due to the reflexion of the water, we are exposed to increased UV radiation while surfing. To protect our skin we apply sunscreen, but what about the eyes? They are often redish and irritated after a long session in the sun, but this is not only due to the salt water – eyes, too, can get sunburned. Just recently the World Health Organization stated that **20 percent of the worldwide blindness is caused by ultraviolet radiation.** The reason for this are so-called free radicals that are created by UV radiation and destroy the cells of skin and eyes. Natural remedies are antioxidants like the plant preservatives lutein, zeaxanthin and astaxanthin which can be found in carrots: They protect your skin's and retina's cells, prevent sunburn and act like natural sunglasses. However, it is not sufficient to just eat one carrot a day. To take in the same amount of antioxidants that we have pressed in a small tab you would need to eat a whole barrow of carrots!"

TRIP PLANNER

Pakistan, China, Egypt and the Black Sea are just a few of the destinations where Frenchman Antony Colas traveled to in search of new waves. Most of the time he scored and came back with exceptional discoveries to tell and share as author of the legendary World Stormrider Guides. There is definitely no one who knows better where to head for a weekend trip, a two-week escape or a surf mission into the unknown...

Weekend Warrior

It's Friday night and you are about to die – you need to surf this weekend, no matter what. So what to do?

"If you have only one weekend to score, there is no sense of heading somewhere and hoping for a swell to arrive. You have to check the surf forecast and know exactly where waves will be firing. Swell chasing is almost always rewarding, just be quick and make sure you hit the right spot at the right time.

In Europe, it often takes only a couple of hours behind the steering wheel or a short flight to get to a perfect wave. **Portugal** is probably the best travel destination in Europe, but **Morocco** is great as well and the **Canary Islands** are almost perfect for a short winter escape.

'Surf is where you find it', said Gerry Lopez, and that's the main thing to understand. Over the years, the Mediterranean Sea has proven to deliver really good surf. During winter times over the last decade, I've done many trips to **Cyprus**, **Malta**, Alexandria in **Egypt**, **Libya**, **Tunisia** or **Algeria**, if the forecast looked good enough. And I've always scored those shores with no one out. For me, the Med is a place of friendly people, great food, fascinating history and really good surf at times. "

Two-Week Escape

Finally, it's vacation time and you have fourteen days to do nothing – or go surfing. But where to find perfect waves?

"Always keep in mind that when you go is more crucial than where you go. If you don't have the freedom to book a last-minute trip to a spot where the forecast looks epic, go somewhere consistent. Maybe a bit out of the peak season, if you want to do your best to avoid crowds. The **Maldives** are a great destination for several reasons: A long season (March – November), consistent Indian Ocean surf, quality long period swells, soft and perfect waves over atoll reefs, crystal clear and warm water, only an overnight flight away, no jet-lag and no diseases.

There are some places like **Hawaii** or **Japan** that do not look so inviting for a trip because of the ratio of waves per surfer. But of all the places I've been to, I would not call one of them hell. It's always cool to be on vacation somewhere and if something goes wrong, then you will have an adventure. In 1996, I went to **Gabon**, got skunked and came back with Falciparum Malaria, but I still think it was a good trip!

Recently, my main surf trips have been to tidal bore waves, especially the Bono in **Sumatra**. Riding such a wave feels a bit different, maybe halfway in between surfing and snowboarding: You race along the river on an endless aquatic ride. The wave is different every day, but swell is guaranteed – so you can't get skunked!

If you are a bit anxious about hassles, dangers and uncertainty, go to a Flow-rider wavehouse, or if you think this is not surfing, try new wavepools like Siam Park in **Tenerife** or the new Wadi Adventure near **Dubai / Abu Dhabi.** You pay 25 euros per hour for 40 waves to share with whoever is there and enjoy a good take off on a 3 to 4ft face wave with enough time for two good moves – it's all trouble free."

Endless Adventure

There are no dates, schedules or booked return tickets - you are free to search our planet and find a spot exclusively for yourself. But how to start?

"On a trip like this it is crucial for you to bear the positive sides of traveling in mind, because you will end up somewhere far from the surf. Maybe because of non-existent transport, a bothering administration, an exotic disease or any other problem you didn't think of when you left home.

If you are up for spending more than a day of traveling to remote places, then there are still lots of spots to surf with no crowds, if any. Last January we went to **Northern Maluku**, where we found quite a few villages to stay

at and surfed virgin waves with just a few naked kids splashing around in the water. Also, **Indonesia** and the **Philippines** are full of cheap options to score waves on your own. The same goes for Africa, which is full of hidden gems! And if you have a budget, there are lots of **islands in the Pacific** or in the **Northern Latitudes** (if you don't mind surfing in cold water) to explore, but such a mission would really require some time and dedication.

Since we have Google Earth it is even more obvious how many spots are still out there to discover. Just think of Surfing magazine's Google Earth Challenge, which brought us the lefts of **Skeleton Point in Africa**, a wave as long as Chicama and barreling like Mundaka."

You want to go on a trip with surfing's most famous globetrotter himself? Antony is offering trips to the Maldives (www.maldivesurf.com) and the tidal wave in Sumatra (www.bonosurf.com)!

May Huey be with you...

THANKS TO...

...all of the experts for sharing their knowledge and time with us.

...Claudius Danesitz who was the source for many of the misfortunes that are told in this book – we have kept some secret for The Surf Trip Survival Guide Vol. 2.

...Gloria Gärtig & Anne Schmidt from Planet Sports for her continuing support.

...our designer and illustrator Daria Malek who has spent sleepless nights to freshen our texts with her art.

...our proofreader and editor Clark Bruce for also reading in between the lines.

PLEASE DO NOT DUMP!

The Surf Trip Survival Guide Survival Bag is 100% recyclable, but shouldn't end up in the trash can. It not only protects the book from salt water, sand and sun, but also collects cigarette butts, coins, cockroaches, sandwiches, travel souvenirs and even saves your life (just read page 86)!

1% of the book's sales will be donated to SurfAid.